Telling Fortunes
with Cards

Telling Fortunes
with Cards

Kevin Martin

COLLIER BOOKS
A Division of Macmillan Publishing Co., Inc.
New York

COLLIER MACMILLAN PUBLISHERS
London

Macmillan Publishing Co., Inc.
866 Third Avenue, New York, N.Y. 10022
Collier Macmillan Canada, Ltd.

Telling Fortunes with Cards was originally published by
A. S. Barnes and Company and is reprinted by arrangement.

Library of Congress Catalog Card Number: 75-107129

First Collier Books Edition 1971
Third Printing 1976

Printed in the United States of America

Contents

Preface

The art of telling fortunes by cards—known as cartomancy—has been practiced for centuries.

In our day and generation divination by cards is chiefly employed for amusement and pastime—for entertaining at a party, church fairs, charity bazaars, and the like—but in the days of the ancients it was practiced by the prophets, sorceresses, and sibyls as a serious business, and so accepted by all, from king to peasant.

Certainly there were some remarkable coincidences—to call them by no other name—in the fulfillment of many cartomantic divinations, of which history maintains a record.

Certainly there is a wonderful fascination in the mastering of cartomancy, in the being able to tell fortunes by the chance falling of the cards into this or that position—and in knowing what each card and grouping is believed to signify.

No prophet or seer ever professed that divination by cards is a natural gift. It is universally recognized as being solely the result of study and practice, and can be mastered by anyone.

Here are the results of centuries of effort on the part of those who profess to believe sincerely in what they practice and teach. You, the reader, are left to place as much or as little credence as you so choose in the truthfulness of their divinations.

Introducing Cartomancy

Joséphine Tascher de la Pagerie (1763-1814), while in her native Martinique, had been approached by an aged Negro woman who astonished her by declaring: "You will ascend upon the loftiest throne in the world."

Always treasuring the memory of this prediction, Joséphine, then the widow of General Beauharnais, during the bitter days of the Reign of Terror, was induced to consult a distinguished seeress of the Faubourg St. Germain. This particular seeress relied upon cartomancy as a means of elucidating the mysteries of the past, present, and future.

Although her visitor was disguised as a waiting woman (a maid or attendant), the seeress, through a simple resort to her pack of cards, correctly read the entire past existence of her consultant.

Then, by the same means, she laid bare the gloomy picture of Joséphine's present situation. She foretold how the prison doors of the Luxembourg stood ready to receive her, and how the guillotine thirsted for her life's blood. She went on to tell Joséphine how, nevertheless, she would be saved from all of these impending dangers through the intercession of a young soldier, a total stranger.

Subsequently, through a fresh appeal to the cards, the seeress was able to throw aside the veil obscuring Joséphine's destiny. She predicted her marriage, and the onward march of her husband, Napoleon, to fame and power. Finally, after a long and studious observation of the cards, the cartomancian announced to her skeptical consultant that on a given day, within the cathedral church of Notre Dame, the unknown man she was destined to marry would place upon her head an imperial diadem, and furthermore that she would be hailed in the presence of the highest ecclesiastical potentate on earth as "Empress of the French," and as such would be respected until her death.

The remarkably rapid and literal fulfillment of the predictions made by a professional seeress to an unknown lady, to whom she promised the most exalted of mortal positions, astonished the crowd of courtiers, wonder-stricken at realization of this indisputable and well-authenticated augury of miraculous events. It also elicited the attention of men of great intellect and of science, hundreds of whom were eventually to visit the prophetess. In every instance they testified to the accuracy of her predictions, although admittedly at a loss to comprehend the source of this apparently superhuman knowledge.

It appeared wonderful to these men of science that the mere combination of a series of cards—which they had always regarded as a mere sort of diversion—could be employed to read the past as well as to penetrate the mysteries of the future. In an elaborate report made to the Emperor—whose comprehensive mind yearned after explanation of all secrets, mental as well as physical— they were compelled to state that, while unable to account for the cause of this prophetic knowledge, there could be no rational doubt of its existence.

This exposition of cartomancy, or the divination by cards, is a complete handbook which thoroughly covers the best authenticated methods of its ancient practice as handed down from the Romany gypsies and the seeresses that antedate them. Different nations and different times had their varying interpretations of the value of each card, and separate and distinct methods of laying the cards for readings. There were, as well, fundamental differences in their interpretations of the many possible combinations of cards. Here you will find a complete symposium of each. The casual reader and the student of the art may now see, learn, and fully understand all the approved methods of the past. He may intelligently choose that method which best pleases or suits his convenience.

All the ancient manuscripts which have been consulted in the preparation of this book insist that divination through playing cards is to be relied upon as a truthful exposition of the past and future, and a veritable portent of the future. Their authors desire to be taken seriously. This author has no desire to detract from this position if it be a fact, nor does he know that it is not a fact.

The would-be cartomancer is advised to study every word of this book in detail, as he would any other lesson he desired to master. Learn the various methods of dealing and of reading the layout. Consult the several interpretations of the meanings and learn how to apply them. Do this at first by reading your own fortune, and later that of friends—this only after you have memorized many of the meanings and have acquired a degree of fluency in elaborating the "talk" or "patter" that goes with a successful reading.

Cartomancy can be mastered by anyone who studies this book, gives the subject some serious thought and sufficient experimental testing to acquire proficiency.

While any ordinary pack of playing cards can be used, it is best to secure, if possible, a pack whose face cards have only a single head. This is because, in dealing, when cards come out reversed, they bear a different signification, in some cases, than when upright.

If, however, the usual double-headed cards are used, it is merely necessary to make a distinctive mark on the top end of the faces of certain ones. This will enable the reader to obtain exactly the same results as with the special fortunetelling pack. The mark may be a simple dot or cross made with a pen or pencil, and should be noted at one end of the card only. So marked, that end will then become the top of the card in all cases. The cards coming out in the deal with this mark at their tops will be considered as upright; with the marked end down, they are reversed.

The only cards that need to be thus distinguished are:

> The face cards of each suit
> The Ace
> The ten of diamonds
> The nine of diamonds
> The eight of diamonds

Spot cards below the seven are in most cases not used. Where they are employed, their reversal has no significance. The top of the seven of diamonds (also the other suits), is considered to be the end that has the extra central pip (spot). Spot cards of the three suits other than diamonds usually require no mark to determine their top or bottom. The "handles" of all spades and clubs, and the apexes of all hearts, point downward when those cards are upright—hence when they point upward the cards are considered as reversed.

If, however, any cards other than those I have mentioned are so printed as to make it difficult to distinguish the top from the bottom, or base, you should carefully mark them at the top.

In some methods of fortunetelling by cards it is essential to have a special card as the representative of the person seeking the response of the oracle. This is commonly called the *Consultant* card. If there is a joker in your pack, or an extra blank card (as is the case in many packs), use one of them as the *Consultant* card. Mark this card distinctly to show which end is its top, as its reversal also has a special signification. If there is neither a joker nor a blank card, use the discarded deuce of any suit in the pack, with a mark at its top end.

Telling Fortunes
with Cards

The Ancient Oracle—
Fifty-two Cards

Various meanings have been ascribed to the individual cards in different countries and times. Several lists—and they are the recognized standards of the art—are given throughout this book. The first list of interpretations is based on a very ancient work, first published around 1600 or a little later. This list, it will be noticed, defines the entire fifty-two cards of the pack and has no separate signification for any card being upright or reversed. Each card retains the identical meaning in either position.

Suit values are generally as follows:

Clubs lead and mostly foretell happiness and good business arrangements. No matter how they are accompanied by cards of other suits, or how numerous, clubs are seldom considered bearers of other than the very best news.
Hearts are next and are usually taken to signify lovemaking, invitations, and good friends.
Diamonds often have to do with money.
Spades predict worry or sickness, annoyances, and sometimes loss of money.

Clubs

ACE: Great wealth, much prosperity, and tranquility of mind.

KING: A humane person, upright and affectionate, faithful in all undertakings, personal happiness, tries to make others happy.

QUEEN: A tender, mild, and rather susceptible woman, who will be extremely attractive to the opposite sex.

JACK: An open, sincere, and good friend, who will exert him- or herself warmly in your behalf.

TEN: Speedy wealth.

NINE: Many disagreeable situations are foreseen in connection with a strongly obstinate nature.

EIGHT: A covetous person, extremely fond of money. Such a person will not make proper use of it.

SEVEN: The most brilliant fortune and the most exquisite bliss this world can give, but beware of the opposite sex, from whom misfortune may come.

SIX: A lucrative partnership.

FIVE: Marriage to a partner who will immensely improve your financial and other circumstances.

FOUR: Inconsistency; radical changes in your life.

TREY: Three wealthy marriages.

DEUCE: Opposition and great disappointment throughout life.

Hearts

ACE: Feasting and pleasure. If accompanied by *spades* it signifies quarreling. If by *hearts* it means friendship and affection. If by *diamonds*, you will hear of an absent friend. If by *clubs*, merrymaking and rejoicing.

KING: A man of good-natured disposition, hot and hasty, rash in his undertakings, and very amorous.

QUEEN: A woman of fair complexion, faithful and affectionate always.

JACK: A person of either sex, but always the dearest friend or closest relative of the consulting party. It is said that you must pay great attention to the cards that stand next to the jack, as from them alone you are supposed to judge whether the person it represents will be favorable to your inclinations or not.

TEN: A good card, for it is supposed to correct the bad tidings of all cards standing next to it. If its neighboring cards are of good tidings, it is supposed to confirm and enhance their value.

NINE: Wealth, grandeur, and high esteem. If cards that are unfavorable stand near it, disappointments and the opposite of wealth and esteem. If favorable cards follow these bad cards, you will retrieve your losses.

EIGHT: Drinking and feasting.

SEVEN: A fickle and unfaithful person.

SIX: A generous, open, credulous disposition, easily imposed upon, but a friend to the distressed and needy.

FIVE: A wavering and unsettled disposition.

FOUR: The person will not be married till quite late in life, simply because he or she is much too particular in making a choice of a mate.

TREY: Your own imprudence will greatly contribute to experiencing much ill will from others.

DEUCE: Extraordinary good future and success. If unfavorable cards accompany this, then it will be delayed for a time.

Diamonds

ACE: A letter will be coming soon.

KING: A man of fiery temper, continued anger, seeking revenge, and extremely stubborn in his convictions.

QUEEN: A flirt, and fond of company. Likes to attract attention.

JACK: However friendly, will look more to their own interests than yours. Easily angered if contradicted, and tenacious in personal opinions.

TEN: A country husband (or wife), with wealth and many children. Very generous with money.

NINE: A surprise about money.

EIGHT: Unhappy marriage late in life.

SEVEN: Waste of things and losses will mar your life.

SIX: An early marriage and widowhood, but a second marriage would probably be worse.

FIVE: Success in enterprises. If married, you will have good children.

FOUR: Vexation and annoyance.

TREY: Quarrels, lawsuits, and domestic disagreements. Your partner in life will be a vixen, bad-tempered, and will make you extremely unhappy.

DEUCE: You will fall in love while very young, but you will meet with great opposition to marriage.

Spades

ACE: Has to do with love affairs, but means death when card is upside down.

KING: An ambitious man, successful in love matters. A great man will befriend him, but let him beware of a serious reversal in his life.

QUEEN: A woman who will be corrupted by the rich of both sexes. A widow.

JACK: A person who, although having your interest at heart, will be too lazy to pursue it.

TEN: Supposedly a card of bad tidings. It will counteract the good effects of the cards near it.

NINE: Professed to be the worst card of the pack. Indicates a total loss of fortune, calamities, and endless contentiousness in your family.

EIGHT: Opposition from your friends. If this card comes out close to you, drop all present plans and develop new ones.

SEVEN: Loss of valuable friend, whose death will greatly distress you.

SIX: Very little success in life or love.

FIVE: Good luck in marriage. Mate will be fond of you. Bad temper and interference will plague you.

FOUR: Much sickness, dangerous disease, sadness.

TREY: Good fortune in marriage, but inconsistent partner will make you very unhappy.

DEUCE: A death or removal by disagreeable means.

Method of Play Using the Foregoing Interpretations

Take a pack of fifty-two cards and shuffle them well at least three times. Make the significator whichever queen you please (if a woman), or a king (if a man). Then proceed to lay them on the table, nine in a row. Wherever the dealer finds himself placed, count nine cards each way, not forgetting the significator. Then it will be seen what card accompanies the significator, and "read" from that.

When several diamonds fall together, the interpretation is that money will soon be received. Several clubs denote drink and noisy, troublesome company. Several spades: trouble and vexation. If two red tens come next to the significator, it means marriage and prosperity. Two red eights indicate new clothes. Interpret the meanings of cards falling on either side of the significator card by consulting the previous list.

If a married woman lays the cards, she must make her husband the king of the same suit of which she is queen—but if she is a single girl, she must make her lover whatever king she may think proper. The jacks of the same suits are supposed to be men's thoughts. You may discover what they are thinking of by counting nine cards from where they are placed. It is said that if a woman wishes to know whether she will obtain her desires in any particular matter or area of interest, let her shuffle the cards well, and most seriously and earnestly wish for that one thing while doing so. She must then cut the cards once, especially observing which card is cut. Then she must shuffle the pack again and deal the cards out in three separate groups. If the cut or "wish" card comes next to her significator queen, or next to the ace of hearts, then she will most certainly get what she desires. But if the nine of spades falls next to her significator, she will be disappointed, because this card is supposed to indicate failure. However, she may try this three times, and then average out the "readings" or interpretations to arrive at an accurate answer.

The Ancient Oracle—
Thirty-two Cards

Many people have striven to fathom divination, or the art of revealing the secrets of the past, present, and future through the aid of cards—but it is to the gypsies one must go if the truth is to be found.

In the following pages, I have given the authentic method of "reading" cards, exactly as handed down to the gypsies of today, and as used in every gypsy encampment.

Usually only eight cards are used, the *ace* ranking highest in value, followed by the *king, queen, knave, ten, nine, eight,* and *seven*.

The individual interpretation attached to each of the cards, according to gypsy lore, is as outlined on the following pages.

The *court* cards of *hearts* and *diamonds* usually represent persons of fair complexion; *clubs* and *spades*, persons of darker complexion.

Clubs

ACE
   Upright: Joy, money, or good news.
   Reversed: The joy will be of brief duration.

KING
   Upright: A frank, liberal man, fond of serving his friends.
   Reversed: He will meet with a major disappointment.

QUEEN
   Upright: An affectionate woman, quick-witted but touchy.
   Reversed: A jealous and malicious woman.

KNAVE
   Upright: A clever and enterprising young man.
   Reversed: A harmless flirt and flatterer.

TEN
   Upright: Fortune, success, or grandeur.
   Reversed: Want of success in some small matter.

NINE
   Upright: Unexpected gain, or a legacy.
   Reversed: Some trifling present.

EIGHT
   Upright: A dark person's affection, which, if returned, will bring great prosperity.
   Reversed: The affections of an undesirable person; unhappiness if reciprocated.

SEVEN
   Upright: A small sum of money, or unexpectedly recovered debt.
   Reversed: An even smaller amount.

Hearts

ACE
   Upright: A love letter, or some pleasant news.
   Reversed: A friend's visit.

KING
   Upright: A fair-skinned, very generous man.
   Reversed: Will run into difficulties.

QUEEN
> *Upright*: A mild-mannered, amiable woman.
> *Reversed*: She has been crossed in love.

KNAVE
> *Upright*: A gay young bachelor who dreams only of pleasure.
> *Reversed*: A discontented military man.

TEN
> *Upright*: Happiness and triumph.
> *Reversed*: Some slight anxiety.

NINE
> *Upright*: Joy, satisfaction, and success.
> *Reversed*: Some slight embarrassment or mortification.

EIGHT
> *Upright*: A fair-complexioned person's affections.
> *Reversed*: Indifference on his or her part.

SEVEN
> *Upright*: Pleasant thoughts, tranquility.
> *Reversed*: Tedium, weariness, languor of spirits.

Diamonds

ACE
> *Upright*: A letter soon to be received.
> *Reversed*: Containing bad news.

KING
> *Upright*: A fair-haired man—generally in the military—cunning and dangerous.
> *Reversed*: A threatened danger, caused by machinations on his part.

QUEEN
> *Upright*: An ill-bred, scandal-loving woman.
> *Reversed*: She is to be greatly feared.

KNAVE

Upright: A tale-bearing servant or unfaithful friend.

Reversed: This person will be the cause of mischief.

TEN

Upright: Journey, or change of residence.

Reversed: The change will not prove fortunate.

NINE

Upright: Annoyance or delay of some sort.

Reversed: Either a family or a love quarrel.

EIGHT

Upright: Lovemaking.

Reversed: Unsuccessful.

SEVEN

Upright: Satire, mockery.

Reversed: A foolish scandal.

Spades

ACE

Upright: Pleasure.

Reversed: Grief, bad news.

KING

Upright: An envious man, a dishonest enemy, a lawyer who is to be feared.

Reversed: Impotent malice.

QUEEN

Upright: A widow.

Reversed: A dangerous and malicious woman.

KNAVE

Upright: A dark, ill-bred young man.

Reversed: He is plotting some mischief.

TEN

Upright: Tears; a prison.

Reversed: A brief affliction.

NINE
Upright: Tidings of death.
Reversed: It will be some close relative.

EIGHT
Upright: Approaching illness.
Reversed: A marriage broken up or an offer refused.

SEVEN
Upright: Slight annoyances.
Reversed: A foolish intrigue.

Cards of the Same Denomination Which Come Together or Fall in Succession

FOUR ACES
Upright: Danger, failure in business, and sometimes imprisonment.
Reversed: If one or more of them are reversed the danger is lessened.

THREE ACES
Upright: Good tidings all around.
Reversed: Foolish actions.

TWO ACES
Upright: A plan or plot.
Reversed: Plot will be unsuccessful.

FOUR KINGS
Upright: Rewards, dignities, honors.
Reversed: They will be less than above, but obtained sooner.

THREE KINGS
Upright: A consultation on important business, the results of which will be extremely satisfactory.
Reversed: Success in the above will be doubtful.

TWO KINGS
Upright: A partnership in business.

Reversed: A dissolution of partnership. This sometimes denotes only friendly projects.

FOUR QUEENS

Upright: Company, visitors, and social activity.

Reversed: The above entertainment will not go off well.

THREE QUEENS

Upright: Friendly visiting and good intelligent conversation.

Reversed: Chattering, gossip, scandal, and deceit.

TWO QUEENS

Upright: A meeting between good friends.

Reversed: Poverty and other troubles which will involve those friends.

FOUR KNAVES

Upright: A noisy party—mostly young people.

Reversed: A heavy drinking spree.

THREE KNAVES

Upright: False friends.

Reversed: A quarrel with some low-class person.

TWO KNAVES

Upright: Evil intentions.

Reversed: Great immediate danger.

FOUR TENS

Upright: Great success in projected enterprises.

Reversed: The success will not be so brilliant, although it will be certain.

THREE TENS

Upright: Improper conduct, some dishonesty.

Reversed: Complete failure in everything.

TWO TENS

Upright: Change of trade or profession.

Reversed: The above prospect is a distant one.

FOUR NINES
Upright: A great surprise.
Reversed: A public dinner.

THREE NINES
Upright: Joy, fortune, and health.
Reversed: Wealth and health lost through imprudence.

TWO NINES
Upright: A little gain.
Reversed: Trifling losses at cards.

FOUR EIGHTS
Upright: A short journey.
Reversed: The return of a friend or relative.

THREE EIGHTS
Upright: Thoughts of marriage.
Reversed: Folly, flirtation.

TWO EIGHTS
Upright: A brief love dream.
Reversed: Small pleasures and trifling pains.

FOUR SEVENS
Upright: Intrigues among low-class people, threats and disputes.
Reversed: Their malice will be impotent and the punishment will fall on themselves. You will not be hurt.

THREE SEVENS
Upright: Sickness and premature old age.
Reversed: Slight and brief indisposition.

TWO SEVENS
Upright: Lack of seriousness, light hearted.
Reversed: Regretful.

Any picture card which comes between two others of equal value—such as two tens, two aces, etc.—denotes that the person represented by that face card is running the risk of a prison term for something he is doing or contemplating.

It requires no great effort to commit these significations to memory. It must be remembered that they are merely what the alphabet is to the printed book. A little attention and practice, however, will soon enable the student to assemble the cards correctly and "read" the events—both past and to come—which the faces reveal. The several methods of doing this are explained in Chapter 4.

Modern Use of Fifty-two Cards—
Interpretations

Here we present the more modern adaptation of the entire pack of fifty-two cards to the fortuneteller's use. Since the meanings differ materially from the ancient list previously given, another complete list is included.

In modern usage, *Diamonds* take precedence and are considered to mean money, riches, and success.

Other suit values are generally as follows:

Hearts are next in importance and indicate love affairs, friendship, amusement and pleasure.

Clubs have to do with business matters, whether investments, appointments, or settlements.

Spades are always indicative of losses or grief, trouble and anxiety, sometimes sickness and death.

The various combinations are supposed to accelerate or else mitigate the several meanings.

For instance, the ace of diamonds coming with the ace of spades, a railway journey; the nine of spades, usually taken to be a bad card, but coming with diamonds, indicates good luck, etc. All various combinations are fully covered in Chapter 7.

Diamonds

ACE: An offer of a ring, usually in terms of an engagement or possibly marriage. But it could be simply out of friendship.

KING: A fair-skinned man, in the military or diplomatic service, will enter into your life for some unknown reason.

QUEEN: A fair-skinned, light-haired woman, passionate and fond of pleasure and amusement. A lover of fun, and one who laughs readily.

JACK: The thoughts of either king or queen.

TEN: A legacy or property.

NINE: A wonderful surprise about money.

EIGHT: Meetings about money matters which should turn out to be most profitable and exciting to all concerned.

SEVEN: A check or paper money; sometimes scandal is involved.

SIX: An offer of some kind, generally having to do with money. Whether profitable or not is another thing.

FIVE: Health, wealth, and supreme happiness. This card is supposed to be the best in the pack.

FOUR: A short journey.

THREE: Time, within three to four weeks. Indicates something is to happen within this period, usually financial.

TWO: A secret or something unexpected is going to happen.

Hearts

ACE: Has something to do with the house.

KING: A fair-skinned man will enter your life for some reason, who is socially prominent and probably in the navy.

QUEEN: A fair-haired, light-complexioned woman who is active socially, and generally kind and good-natured.

JACK: The thoughts of either king or queen.

TEN: Some sort of entertainment or festivity. Possibly a party, club activity, or even just a movie.

NINE: Great happiness is in store. This card is called the wish card, for if you wish something, it is bound to come true.

EIGHT: Lovemaking or a close friendship will play an important role in your life. How it turns out is another question.

SEVEN: A puzzle or indecision and doubt will enter your mind over something of great importance to your future.

SIX: Love affairs, sometimes an offer. Whether this is a marriage offer is doubtful, it could well be that.

FIVE: Marriage; sometimes a new admirer. Whether you like this person or not is another question. Opportunity will be presented.

FOUR: A small invitation, such as a dinner or an evening party, will be sent you soon. You should try to attend.

THREE: Time, within a week, something will happen that will concern you.

TWO: Kisses or a trifling present will be offered to you.

Clubs

ACE: A letter of some sort.

KING: A clever, dark-complexioned man, often a professional person or one in business for himself.

QUEEN: A clever, extremely amusing and well-liked woman, who is sometimes a little satirical.

JACK: The thoughts of either king or queen.

TEN: A new appointment, investment, or settlement. Something important is going to take place in your business life.

NINE: Relates to documents, papers, often a will. Whether beneficial or not is another question.

EIGHT: A journey by road or vehicle. It might even be a trip by jet to some far-off land.

SEVEN: A warning or unprofitable business venture.

SIX: A very poor business offer, one that would not do you any good to accept. It also might mean borrowed money.

FIVE: News, either from the country or from some person who now lives in the country. Could be a telephone call of importance.

FOUR: A journey by land on business matters. May or may not be profitable for you in the end, but you must go nevertheless.

THREE: Time; within three to four months, something is going to take place.

TWO: A good friend will become more deeply involved in your life. In some cases this indicates a slight disappointment.

Spades

ACE: Spite, death, hatefulness, contempt, cruelty, jealousy, and worry. Sometimes a large town.

KING: A lawyer who is very old and a widower. He is very dark-complexioned, with dark eyes and hair.

QUEEN: A spiteful, malicious, detestful, arrogant woman who is very dark and a widow of recent date. She means trouble.

JACK: The thoughts of either king or queen.

TEN: At nighttime, imprisonment for some reason.

NINE: Grief, suffering, malice; and with other black cards, death. This card is always supposed to be extremely bad.

EIGHT: Across water, sometimes treachery is involved. In any case, be on guard with this card.

SEVEN: Poverty will befall you or someone close to you. There is much anxiety and annoyance in store.

SIX: Delays will crop up in every undertaking, or you will become deeply involved with someone of extremely bad character.

FIVE: Temper, anger, and quarrels will mar your future to a large degree. It cannot be avoided.

FOUR: Sickness, sometimes a trip as a result of sickness. It could be your own illness or someone else's.

THREE: By the water, or a very short trip across water.

TWO: Tears and vexation, sometimes an operation.

The English Method

In England, the entire pack of fifty-two cards is normally used in fortunetelling. Very few other countries still prefer using the whole pack. The significations differ in many cases from those previously given, so I have added this list to show their special interpretations. In this case, *clubs* take precedence and are followed by *diamonds, hearts*, and *spades*, in that order.

Clubs

ACE: Wealth, happiness, and peace of mind.

KING: A dark man, upright, faithful and affectionate, with a good disposition.

QUEEN: A dark woman, gentle and pleasing.

KNAVE: A sincere but hasty friend. Also a dark man's thoughts.

TEN: Unexpected riches and the loss of a dear friend.

NINE: Disobedience to a friend's wishes.

EIGHT: A warning against speculation. Also a covetous man.

SEVEN: Good fortune, but beware of the opposite sex.

SIX: A lucrative business.

FIVE: A prudent marriage.

FOUR: Cautions against inconsistency. Don't change objectives just for money.

THREE: Will marry more than once.

TWO: A great disappointment.

Diamonds

ACE: A letter—neighboring cards will tell from where and why.

KING: A fair-complexioned man—hot-tempered, obstinate, and vengeful.

QUEEN: A fair-complexioned woman, flirty and enjoys company.

KNAVE: A selfish close relative. A fair person's thoughts.

TEN: Money.

NINE: A restless person, fond of moving around.

EIGHT: A marriage late in life.

SEVEN: Satirical and evil-speaking.

SIX: Early marriage and widowhood.

FIVE: Unexpected news.

FOUR: A betrayed secret, trouble with unfaithful friends.

THREE: Quarrels, lawsuits, and domestic disagreements.

TWO: An engagement against the wishes of friends.

Hearts

ACE: The house. If attended by hearts it means affection and friendship. If by spades, it denotes quarreling.

KING: A fair-complexioned man, good-natured but hasty and rash.

QUEEN: A fair-complexioned woman, faithful, prudent, and loving.

KNAVE: The dearest friend of the consulting party. Also a fair person's thoughts.

TEN: Happiness and many children. This card is corrective of bad tidings from adjacent cards, and confirms the good ones.

NINE: Wealth and high esteem. Also the "wish" card.

EIGHT: Pleasure, company.

SEVEN: A fickle and false friend against whom you should be on guard.

SIX: A generous but gullible person.

FIVE: Troubles caused by unfounded jealousy.

FOUR: A person not easily convinced.

THREE: Sorrow caused by a person's own imprudence.

TWO: Great success, but care and attention needed to get it.

Spades

ACE: Great misfortune and spite.

KING: A dark-complexioned, ambitious man.

QUEEN: A malicious, dark-complexioned woman. Generally a widow.

KNAVE: A lazy, envious person. Also a dark man's thoughts.

TEN: Grief, imprisonment.

NINE: A card of very bad import, foretells sickness and misfortune.

EIGHT: Be cautious in your undertakings. A serious warning.

SEVEN: Loss of a friend. Much trouble in store over this.

SIX: Wealth through hard conscientious work.

FIVE: Shows that a bad temper needs correcting.

FOUR: Sickness.

THREE: A journey.

TWO: A removal.

Modern Use of Fifty-two Cards—
Twelve Methods of Dealing

Method One

A pack of fifty-two cards is taken, shuffled, and cut in three sections. The first ten are taken out, and then three are missed. Another nine are taken out, and two are missed. Another seven are taken out, and five are missed. Another seven are taken out, and three are missed. Another three are taken out, and one missed. Then the last cards are taken.

The cards are now laid out in rows of eight each— eight having been counted every way, beginning from the significator card. When all are finished, the two extremities are taken, paired, and "read."

They are then gathered together, shuffled, and cut into four parcels. The first card of each parcel is taken off and put on one side. The packet that comes first is the one which should be "read."

Method Two

A pack of fifty-two cards is taken, shuffled and cut in three sections, each meaning being "read" as it turns up. The cards are then turned up one by one until a spade is found. This spade is not to be withdrawn, but the card which follows it is withdrawn and laid face up on the table. If three spades are found in succession, the first is missed, but the next two are taken out, as well as the following card, whether diamonds, clubs, or hearts.

This procedure is continued until the end of the pack is reached. Then recommence without shuffling or cutting. Should the final card have been a spade, on beginning afresh the first card should be taken out. This same operation is gone through twice more, three times in all.

Having done this, you now lay the cards in the form of a horseshoe in front of you, in the order in which they come. Be careful to note that the significator is amongst them. Should it not appear naturally, it must be taken out and placed at the end.

Seven are now counted from the one representing the person consulting the oracle. When they have been "read," and the relative meanings ascribed to them explained, one is taken from each end and paired. Their various significations are to be interpreted as they are turned up. These prognostications are supposed to come to pass within two months.

A shorter method can be utilized by taking out thirty-two selected cards, that is, the ace, king, queen, jack, ten, nine, eight, and seven of each suit. They are "read" in precisely the same manner. This method is used to allow a shorter time period to elapse—from ten to fourteen days—but the former method is supposed to be the better of the two.

Method Three

A pack of fifty-two cards is taken, and after being well shuffled, they are turned up one by one as you count one, two, three, four, five, six, seven, eight, nine, ten, jack, queen, king (here the ace counts as one). If any card should fall on the particular number counted—thus, supposing a five comes up when five is counted, or a king when that card turns up—it must be taken out and placed on the table, face up, before the dealer. After counting to a king, the counting is recommenced at one.

Should two cards follow—such as a three and a four, eight and nine, etc.—these must be extracted. Any three of a kind, such as three tens, three kings, etc., must also be taken out. If three cards, such as a three, four, and five, etc., are of the same suit, they may be passed by. But if they are not, then they too must be pulled out.

When the pack has been carefully gone through, shuffled, and cut the process is repeated twice more—three times in all. All the cards are now laid out in rows of four and "read." When this is done, they are gathered together and laid two by two, thus:

NORTH

WEST   EAST

SOUTH

Count the cards one, two, three, four, five, six, seven, eight, nine, ten, eleven, twelve, thirteen, fourteen, fifteen, sixteen, and so on until the entire pack is exhausted. Those at the top are the NORTH, those at the bottom are the SOUTH, those on the right hand the EAST and those on the left hand the WEST. The NORTH is to be "read" first, as that is supposed to happen first. Then "read" the SOUTH next, EAST after that, and WEST last.

Method Four

The pack of fifty-two cards is taken, shuffled, and then cut in three sections. The meanings of the cuts are to be "read" first. Then the significator card is taken out. The cards are spread on the table, dealt face down, and seven are drawn out at random. The topmost card of the seven is taken off and put to one side.

The cards are again shuffled and cut in three sections, the cuts again "read" as before. They are laid on the table—seven cards again being taken off—the topmost withdrawn and as before laid to one side.

This is to be repeated a third time, still taking off the topmost card. The cards are again shuffled and cut, now *nine* each time being drawn out and the topmost *two* removed. This maneuver is done three times, always taking out two of the top cards.

In the first deal, where the first seven cards were removed, there will be eighteen cards. The second time there will be twenty-one left after removing two from each cut.

Then, the thirty-nine cards are spread out in five rows of seven, and the four remaining are placed underneath. The significator card is now put in the center, and counting every way from it, these cards are taken to signify the past and the present. The nine cards which have been taken from each of the previous seven and nine draws are to be shuffled and looked at. These are supposed to refer entirely to the future. The four cards which had been placed underneath, or left out, are disregarded as of no value to the consultant.

Method Five

The pack of fifty-two cards is taken, shuffled, and cut in three sections. Each cut is explained or interpreted as it is shown. The card representing the significator should be taken out and placed in the middle, on the table in front of the dealer. Three cards are now placed above the head of the center or significator card. Then follow this with three at the feet, three to the left, three to the right, three at each of the four corners, and three across the significator. They are to be interpreted as follows: First "read" those above the head, then those at the feet, then to the right hand, and next to the left hand. Then take either of the two top corners, and after "reading" the meanings, proceed to the opposite lower corner. Follow this by "reading" the other top corner cards and then again the other opposite lower corner. When these cards are all explained (those across the significator being "read" last), they are then paired, beginning with the topmost cards and the bottom cards, from end to end. Then "read" the combination interpretations.

Method Six

There is a much shorter way of performing the above. Instead of placing the cards as they come, first shuffle them well and lay them face down on the table. Withdraw nine cards (the significator must be in the center). In this method, the nine withdrawn cards are placed around the significator (card representing the consultant), in the order in which they come. In other words, the first card taken from the nine is put at the head of the significator or center card, the next at the feet, and so on as explained above. Then the nine cards are "read" or explained in rotation, eight around to the right or left, starting of course with the card at the head and finishing with the one placed over the significator in the center.

Then the consulter is to again draw nine more cards, these nine being placed directly over the first nine. Follow with a "reading" and then repeat exactly the same procedure a third time. When completed, there will be three cards in each pile, laid upon the other, three deep. Take each pile individually and combine the meanings of the three cards in it. This will constitute your fourth and final "reading."

Method Seven

The whole pack is taken, shuffled well, but not cut. Then go through the deck and remove every fifth card and lay them aside in one pile. Follow this by again going through the deck and removing every seventh card. These too are set aside in a separate stack. Finally, go through the deck and take every third card and place them in a separate pile. Then examine the three separate piles to see if the significator card is among those withdrawn. If not, then it must be located and taken from the deck and then placed at the extreme end. Now lay the third pack (the pile of every third card previously drawn) out in a row, the second (the stack of every seventh card) next, and the first (the pile of every fifth card) last.

Beginning with the significator, count three, seven, and five down each row, and all that is hidden is said to be revealed to you. Now take one from each end of all three rows and give a "reading" on these six cards. Do this a second time and set all twelve cards to one side. Then the rest of the cards are picked from end to end in the same manner, and "read" until all are exhausted. Follow this by picking up all the cards so used (including the twelve set aside), and shuffle them well once again. The first two cards and the last single card are taken off the deck. These three cards form the "surprise." Then parcels of four are dealt, beginning with the first. Each parcel is "read" in rotation and the "surprise" cards are "read" last.

Method Eight

The pack of fifty-two cards is taken, shuffled, and cut in three sections. Explain the meaning of each of the three cut cards which are shown. Then take the entire pack and count off rows of five cards each until it is exhausted. The first row (to the left) is to represent "the person for whom you are acting." The second denotes "the house," the third "your wish," the fourth "the surprise," and the fifth "what is supposed to come true."

The first ten cards are now "read" *lengthwise*, or from left to right, starting with the ten closest to the dealer. Do all the others in the same manner until reaching and explaining or "reading" the fifth row. Then take the card from each end of every row and interpret these pairs. In other words, pick up the first and last card of every row and pair them. In this case there is no significator card, since the first row is supposed to stand for what will happen immediately to the consultant.

Then gather all the cards together, shuffle well, cut and lay in packets of three. The consulter must select any one of the three packets, which is then laid out as above, in rows of five, and explained or "read." The other two packets follow the same procedure.

Method Nine

The pack of fifty-two cards is taken, shuffled, and cut by the person consulting. They are cut in three ways and the meanings interpreted. Then they are laid out in seven rows of seven cards each. The last three are discarded. Locate the significator card and count nine from it in every direction, backward and forward, from left to right and up and down, always coming back to it. Then the cards are paired from corner to corner, each card being explained as it is arrived at. Note particularly if there are any pairs, triplets, or four of a kind among the cards, and if so interpret their combined meanings.

Then gather all the cards together again, shuffle well, and deal in two packets. The consultant is to select from one of these packets. The one chosen is supposed to represent the past and present, the other denotes the future. They are laid out and "read" pretty much as before.

Method Ten

A pack of fifty-two cards is taken, shuffled, and cut, and then divided in the following manner. Every nine, seven, and five spot are removed and put to one side. The six of clubs, the eight of diamonds, and the ten of diamonds are also withdrawn and put in a place by themselves. The rest are then shuffled and laid out in rows of five cards each, face up, until the pack is exhausted. It will now be found that there are seven rows of five cards each and two cards left over. These two left-overs are to be placed with the nines, sevens, and fives for later use.

To "read" these cards, count seven every way from the significator card. After completing the "readings," withdraw the first group or row of seven from the table and add these to the nines, sevens, and fives already withdrawn. Then gather the other four rows together, shuffle well and cut, and place in four rows of seven cards each.

The first row must be "read," the second put aside, the third "read," and the fourth laid aside. The second and fourth rows are left out entirely and not used from here on out.

The nines, sevens, and fives and the first group of seven you have withdrawn are shuffled, cut into two packets, and laid out on the table before the dealer. If *two red nines* appear close together, it is taken to show honor, dignity, and joy. If *two red sevens* and *two red fives* are side by side it denotes great and unexpected good luck, a legacy or money which was not anticipated and general financial gain. *Two red fives* and the *nine of hearts* near each other represent a very loving marriage, while if with the *seven of diamonds*, it represents a marriage for money, but still with some love in the background. If *two red fives* and *two black sevens* appear near each other, then you have a marriage for money and an unhappy one. If *two red sevens, two red fives*, and the *nine of hearts* appear, it is supposed to be the greatest and happiest sign you can have, whether married or single, for it indicates luck, pleasure, and money —all in great abundance.

If *two black sevens* and *two black fives* appear, it is considered very evil. If accompanied by the *nine of spades*, it forebodes something even worse and tells of unhappiness in marriage, divorce, scandal, and sometimes violence caused through drink. If the *eight of spades* should be among those withdrawn and turn up with the aforesaid cards, violent death by accident or murder is probable. This combination is taken to be the worst possibility in the entire pack.

These cards (the nine, seven, and five spots, and those that have been withdrawn from the group previously) are laid in rows of sevens by counting seven every way from the significator. Then the extreme end cards are taken and paired, and "read" as they are turned up.

Next the whole is shuffled, including the six of clubs and the eight of diamonds and ten of diamonds (which were set aside separately in the beginning). These three cards act as an index. Wherever they appear, they are supposed to show good luck, happiness, and general prosperity. If they happen to come between exceptionally bad cards, the luck is over, or at least marred through carelessness. But as a general rule, these index cards are taken to represent great joy.

The evil combination is thus: If the *six of clubs* is surrounded by *spades*, or the *eight of diamonds* or *ten of diamonds* is between *two black fives*, and *two black sevens* are near, the best planned venture will turn out for the worst. But if they are surrounded by the *nine of hearts* and the *nine of diamonds*, the omen is very good. The *eight of diamonds* and the *ten of diamonds* are supposed to be extremely good if there are *three* or *four nines* to follow them, for the *nine of spades* loses its evil significance. Should the *seven of diamonds* and the *seven of hearts* follow, a good marriage and great happiness is certain. Or, if the person is already married, then new prosperity or riches for the husband and sometimes the birth of an heir is in store.

Method Eleven

The pack of fifty-two cards is taken, shuffled and cut, and divided into two equal groups. One of these piles is chosen by the consultant. This having been decided, the other pile is disregarded.

The person consulting must now shuffle the chosen twenty-six cards and cut them three times. The meanings are "read" as they turn up.

The cards are then dealt in three stacks, which are laid out in rows of eight. The last card is to be left out, as that forms the "surprise." Should the significator card not be in the pack chosen, it is removed from the other pack of twenty-six and put at the end. Four cards are now counted in every direction from the significator. When these cards (every fourth one), are all explained or "read," the "surprise" card is turned up and also "read." Then the cards are gathered up, shuffled again, and the maneuver is repeated twice (three times in all). One card is always taken out for the "surprise."

Then they are all gathered up together, and after being shuffled and cut, they are turned up by fours. The dealer now lays them out in a row and "reads" them from left to right of the significator. Always make certain that the significator card is among them, and count four from that point as described above. If a sequence should come up, such as six and seven, or six, seven, and eight of any suit, they are to be taken out. If four of a suit show up, take the lowest card out.

Two cards are taken from each extremity and paired, each pair being explained or "read" until the cards are exhausted. This procedure is to be done just once.

Method Twelve

A pack of fifty-two cards is taken, shuffled well, and cut. It is then divided into three equal stacks of seventeen cards each. The one card left over is for the "surprise," which is to be set aside for later. The first three cards of each packet are taken and each group of three is placed in a separate pile, so that now we have fourteen cards in each major group.

Now take up the first and third packets of fourteen and put the middle one aside. These two groups of fourteen are now laid out in four horizontal rows of seven each. Be sure that the significator card is among them—

or else the card which is supposed to represent the
thoughts of the person consulting you (the jack) may
be counted from.

Now count six beginning from the card next to the
significator, and "read" the card's meaning. Then start
from the card following the sixth one and count six
again. Continue this process until you have returned to
the significator. When every sixth card has been explained or "read," then the end cards of each row are
paired and "read."

Gather the cards together again, shuffle and cut, and
divide once more into groups of fourteen. These cards
are not to be laid out again. Merely extract two cards
from each of these new groups of fourteen and also two
more cards from the middle one which was set aside.
Add these six cards to the three packets of three cards,
each which was placed to one side earlier. They now
will each total five.

The middle group of fourteen is now taken up and
shuffled well. Take four cards from it, two from the top
and two from the bottom. Add these four new cards to
the *one* formerly put aside to form the "surprise."

There are now four packets of five cards each. One
is for the "consultant," one for the "house," one for
"what is sure to come true," and one for the "surprise."
These are laid out in front of the dealer and "read" from
left to right in rotation.

Modern Use of Thirty-two Cards—
Primary Interpretations

We now come to the most important and approved modern method of telling fortunes by playing cards, the method preferred and practiced in nearly all countries. This widely accepted method requires but thirty-two of the fifty-two-card pack. These consist of eight cards from each suit, as follows: king, queen, jack, ace, ten, nine, eight, and seven, in that order of importance. To these may be added, in some cases, the *consultant* card, which was mentioned in the Introduction.

To enable this oracle to be read with an intelligent and proper understanding, it is important to be fully informed about all the possible values or interpretations of the cards, singly or in combination. Several pages are devoted to these definitions in very complete form. The simple and primary interpretations are given initially, followed in detail by their secondary or synonymical meanings in Chapter 6, and the interpretation of groups and combinations in Chapter 7. The information in these three chapters constitutes a valuable reference for all who practice the art, for it enables them to give a full, fair, and wise "reading" of every possible "fall" of the cards. These interpretations should be read, understood,

and remembered before you proceed to the various
methods of dealing, laying, and "reading" the cards
covered in Chapter 8.

Diamonds

KING

>   *Upright*: Marriage. A military man. A man of fidelity.
>   A dignitary of state. A very fair-complexioned per-
>   son. A man of tact and cunning.
>
>   *Reversed*: A country gentleman. A difficulty concern-
>   ing marriage or business. Threatened danger, from
>   a man of high position or political office.

QUEEN

>   *Upright*: A blond female. A lady resident in the
>   country. A woman who always gossips and creates
>   scandals.
>
>   *Reversed*: A country gentlewoman. A malicious,
>   troublesome female, who seeks to create difficulties
>   for the consultant. She is to be greatly feared and
>   avoided if at all possible.

JACK

>   *Upright*: A country man. A young man of light com-
>   plexion, of a lower class socially. A messenger.
>   Postman. A tale-bearing, unfaithful friend.
>
>   *Reversed*: A servant. A meddler who will cause prob-
>   lems. A bearer of bad news.

ACE

>   *Upright*: A letter, a petition, a note, a paper, a doc-
>   ument to come after a lapse of time.
>
>   *Reversed*: A letter, a petition, a note, a paper, a
>   document to arrive shortly.

TEN

>   *Upright*: Bullion, coin, gold, water, the sea or ocean,
>   a foreign city, a journey and a change in location.

Reversed: Same as above.

NINE

Upright: Enterprise. Separation. Advantage.

Reversed: Delay. Annoyance. Poverty. A family feud. A quarrel among intimate friends.

EIGHT

Upright: The country. Riches. Lovemaking overtures.

Reversed: Sorrow. Motion. Wealth. Mockery and foolish scandal.

SEVEN

Upright: Present intentions. Good news. A time of joy and laughter.

Reversed: Birth. Contrariness. Vexation. A great deal of displeasure.

Hearts

KING

Upright: A blond man. A lawyer. A man of repute, and one remarkable for superior qualities. A very generous person.

Reversed: A very fair-complexioned man. A teacher. A man capable of great anger. A man who is presently irritated. Deep disappointment.

QUEEN

Upright: A blond female. A very faithful friend. A mild-mannered lady. One who always seems to be amiable.

Reversed: A very fair-haired female. Impediment to marriage. Obstacle to business success and other affairs in general. A woman crossed in love.

JACK

Upright: A blond young man. A young soldier or sailor. A traveler. A gay young bachelor who dreams chiefly of his own pleasures. A man who cannot be taken seriously in love.

Reversed: A very fair young man. A dissipated bachelor. A disgruntled military man. A politician out of office.

ACE

Upright: The house. A feast or meal of some sort. Great festivity. A love letter. Agreeable, intelligent conversation.

Reversed: A good friend's visit. Forced or constrained enjoyment.

TEN

Upright: The city. Envious people. Jealousy and indiscretion.

Reversed: An inheritance. A wonderful surprise.

NINE

Upright: Victory. Ultimate happiness. Triumph. Union. Harmony. Work. Trade. An exciting gift.

Reversed: Weariness. Discontent. Boredom. A passing problem. Curiosity. Encumbrances. Unlooked for responsibility.

EIGHT

Upright: The affection of a fair-complexioned young lady. Success in everything you undertake. Nourishment. Food. Board.

Reversed: A very fair maiden. Excessive joy. A young woman's indifference to your love advances.

SEVEN

Upright: The thoughts. A weapon. A jewel. Something of great value.

Reversed: Strong desire. A parcel or package. A surprise.

Spades

KING

Upright: A dark-visaged man. A gentleman of a learned profession. A judge. Surgeon. Doctor. A literary man. An artist.

Reversed: A widower. A man in wrath or disposed to malice. An envious man. A shyster lawyer. A quack. An enemy. General failure in all your goals and plans.

QUEEN

Upright: A dark woman. A widow. A lady of some highly regarded profession.

Reversed: A widow seeking to marry again. A dangerous and malicious woman. A promiscuous female. Difficulty. Problems in marriage.

JACK

Upright: A dark-complexioned bachelor. A messenger. An ill-bred fellow. Rather low-type admirer.

Reversed: An inquisitive, impertinent intruder. A man plotting mischief. A troublemaker to be avoided. A spy. Pursuit. Treason in love affairs.

ACE

Upright: Abandonment. A document.

Reversed: Pregnancy. Abandonment. Grief. Distressing information or news.

TEN

Upright: Tears, unhappiness, and jealousy. An unexpected break of an engagement or marriage.

Reversed: Loss. An evening party. Brief affliction. In the evening.

NINE

Upright: A great loss. Tidings of death. Mourning a friend or relative. Complete failure in a certain undertaking.

Reversed: Disappointment. Delay. Desertion when least expected. Tidings of the death of a very close relative.

EIGHT

Upright: Sickness. Lack of prudence. Bad news. Much sadness.

Reversed: Ambition. A religious woman. A marriage ending in divorce. An offer of marriage refused.

SEVEN

Upright: Great expectation. Hope for something good. A better future in store. Much happiness in the offing.

Reversed: Wise counsel. Friendship. Indecision. A foolish intrigue. Feel regretful for actions.

Clubs

KING

Upright: A man of medium complexion. Fair-haired. A frank, open-minded person. A good friend. Trustworthy. Dependable. Honesty and virtue.

Reversed: A nut-brown man. A person to meet with a great disappointment and failure for a time.

QUEEN

Upright: A brunette. One fond of conversation but often talks too much for her own good. An affectionate, quick-tempered woman. A kind and loving disposition.

Reversed: A nut-brown woman or girl. A jealous and malicious female. A frustrated lady.

JACK

Upright: A somewhat dark young man. May be well tanned. A bachelor and a lover. A clever and enterprising young fellow. Has a long smooth line for the ladies and can't be relied upon.

Reversed: A flirt and a flatterer who plays the game of love with insincerity. A young man who is angry. One who is ill.

ACE

Upright: A purse full of money. Great wealth.

Reversed: Nobility. Love. A present.

TEN

Upright: The house. The future. Fame. Fortune. Success. Material gain. Money. Wonderful luck in everything.

Reversed: A little money. A lover. Sometimes will be unsuccessful in trivial matters.

NINE

Upright: A mortgage on personal property. Material goods. Movable articles. An indiscretion. Lack of proper attention.

Reversed: A trifling present. Gambling.

EIGHT

Upright: The affections of a brunette maiden. The art of pleasing.

Reversed: A nut-brown maiden. Removal. Separation. A frivolous courtship. A breaking-off of all relations.

SEVEN

Upright: A small sum of money. A debt unexpectedly paid. A small child. A major surprise. Small investment.

Reversed: A small child. Great embarrassment. Many problems will arise.

The Consultant Card

When it comes out in an upright position, in the body of the deal: It merely designates that the person consulting the oracle is in a natural state of mind and clear-headed.

When the card comes out reversed in the deal: It denotes that the consultant is in a disturbed state of mind, or annoyed from some cause beyond his or her control.

Coming with the eight of spades reversed, for example, by its side: It shows that the consultant's mind has been disordered through religious excitement or from having an overpowering yet frustrated ambition.

If accompanied by the eight of hearts: It demonstrates that he or she is annoyed through being a recent victim of tender passion.

Modern Use of Thirty-two Cards—
Secondary Interpretations

The primary meanings, covered in Chapter 5, although sufficient for the amateur, will soon be seen by the student to be lacking in that completeness and flexibility demanded by the adept. Their natural amplification into their secondary and more extended definitions gives the interpreter the fullest scope to exercise his or her power of intelligently "reading" any possible layout of the cards, and with satisfaction to him or herself and to the person consulting the oracle.

Diamonds

KING

Upright: This card, when used as a representative, denotes a very fair man, one with auburn hair, light blue eyes and a florid complexion, who, notwithstanding a hasty temper, will hide his anger. He waits long and patiently for revenge and is stubborn once his mind is made up.

Moreover, it designates a military officer, one who is extremely patriotic and loyal to his country, and a man of honor.

Yet the king is more generally employed as the marriage card, for if it does not come out in an oracle wherein matrimony is the wish, the nuptials will be delayed or broken off.

The synonymical signification would then be: Alliance, reunion, attachment, vow, oath, intimacy, assemblage, junction, union, chain, peace, accord, harmony, understanding, and reconciliation.

Reversed: This card signifies a country gentleman, in which capacity its synonyms are: Country man, rustic, villager, peasant, farm laborer, cultivator, rural and agriculture.

Again, this card reversed bears a further signification of a good and severe man. Its synonyms would be: Indulgent severity, indulgence, complacency, tolerance, low descension.

When used as the marriage card, and coming out reversed, the king of diamonds signifies difficulties and obstacles placed in the way of entering upon or consummating the nuptial contract, and through inference vitiation of the married state, when its synonyms are: Slavery, servitude, matrimonial rupture, and conjugal infidelity.

QUEEN

Upright: When this card comes out in the oracle upright it bears three primary significations: *A country lady, a talkative* or *communicative female*, and a *good, kind-hearted woman*.

As a representative card it designates a very fair female with auburn or blond hair, brilliantly clear complexion, and blue eyes. A woman of this character is socially inclined and a natural flirt.

When the card is taken as *a country lady*, its synonyms will be through induction or inference: Economical housewife, chaste and honest woman, civility, politeness, honesty, sweetness of temper, virtue, honor, virginity, a model wife, excellent mother.

When used to denote *a talkative female*, they will be: Conversation, discourse, deliberation, dissertation, discussion, conference, intellectual entertainment, prattler, blab, idle talk, gossip, flippant conversation, table talk.

Reversed: When this card comes out reversed in the oracle its ordinary signification is that of a meddlesome woman who has interfered with the affairs of the consultant for the purpose of doing him or her injury. The extent of the injury, contemplated or done, can be estimated from the proximity of this card to that of the consultant, or from the import of those cards intervening between the two. This card has two secondary significations: *want of foresight* and *a knavish trick.*

When this card is taken as *want of foresight*, its synonyms are: Unaware, unexpected, napping, sudden, astonished, unhoped for, fortuitous, surprising.

When used to denote a *knavish trick*, they will be: Roguishness, knavery, cheat, deceit, impostor, rascal, trickery, false, pretense, wile, craftiness, artifice, and liar.

JACK

Upright: The primary signification of this card is *a soldier, a horseman*, or a light-haired *young man, in or from the country*. In addition to these characteristics this card, whether upright or reversed, assumes another, which is technically termed *the good stranger*.

As a *soldier*, its secondary value is expressed in the following synonyms: Man at arms, swordsman, fencing master, combatant, enemy, duel, war, battle, attack, defense, opposition, resistance, courage, ruin, overthrow, hostility, hatred, wrath, resentment, valor, bravery, professional fighter.

In the quality of *the good stranger*, its synonyms are: Strange, unaccustomed, unknown, unheard of, surprising, admirable, marvelous, prodigious, miracle, episode, digression, anonymous.

When employed as a representative of a person, it denotes a light-haired, unmarried man who, through one of your closest relatives, will sacrifice your interests to his own. He is stubborn, hasty, hot-headed, impulsive, tenacious, and unable to take criticism.

Reversed: This card's signification is a public or private servant—and in the latter case, without reference to gender, either a male or female domestic. Its synonyms therefore are in accordance with its acceptance: Servant, waiter, valet, chambermaid, a subordinate, an inferior, a hireling, condition of one employed, servitude, postman, errand boy, messenger, agent, expressman, newsman, message, announcement, a household, commission, directions, in relation to the post office and the transmission of messages.

ACE

Upright or reversed: It is a matter of utter indifference whether this card assumes its place in the oracle in an upright or reversed position, as its primary signification is in no way varied.

It requires, however, a great deal of attention to discriminate between the manifold significations of this all-important card, which is governed in large measure by the cards placed next to it. Otherwise the interpreter may be entirely baffled by the intent of the oracle.

The general synonyms of the *ace of diamonds* are: Epistle, writings, grammar, Holy Writ, text, literature, doctrine, erudition, literary labor, book, correspondence, composition, alphabet, elements of all learning, principles, bonds, bills of exchange, notes, evidence of indebtedness.

With the *seven of spades*, reversed, coming next to it, this card denotes the existence of a lawsuit, in which case we have synonyms founded on the following basis: Deed, covenant, agreement, legal document, writs, warrants, litigation, differences, contestations, disputes, discussions, bickering, contest, strife, discord, contradiction, trick, embroglio, stratagem, wrangling.

TEN

Upright or reversed: Like its companion, the *ace*, which with this card forms the only two in the pack possessing this special quality, the *ten of diamonds* preserves its value and signification whether it emerges upright or reversed. The primary significations of this card are *gold, water, the sea, a foreign city, change of locality*.

As the representative of *gold* its synonyms are: Riches, opulence, magnificence, splendor, sumptuousness, luxury, abundance, means.

When its signification is assumed in relation to *water* and the *sea*, the synonyms assume both a specific and general nature: Fluid, humid, dew, rain, deluge, the ocean, river, torrent, stream, fountain, source, leak, lake, pond, cascade, falls.

When the surrounding cards designate the ten to be accepted as representing a *foreign city*, its synonyms are: Traveler, traveling, foreign ports, beyond the sea, homeless, wanderer, wandering abroad, trading, commerce, a sailor, ships, exile.

When accepted to signify a *change in locality*, the synonyms, in addition to preserving its original meaning of a mere change in domicile, or habitation, are inferentially extended to embrace a wider scope, such as: Departure, displacement, journey, pilgrimage, steps, motion, visits, excursions, emigration, immigration, transmigration, flight, tour, rotation, circulation, deportation, rout, overthrow, bewilderment, disconcert, to break an allegiance, desertion, alien, a foreigner, disinheritance, alienation, homeless.

It will be seen that with the varied significations which can be given to this card, it is one of the most important in the pack.

NINE

Upright: When coming forth in its natural position, this card is one of especially good omen. It foretells great success in business operations and consequent gain. Its primary meaning comprehends the grand mainspring to human exertion, *enterprise*, while at the same time it assures you of the desired result—*advantage* or *gain*. Viewed as such, its synonyms are, as to *enterprise* in the first instance: To undertake, to commence, to usurp, to take possession of, audacity, boldness, imprudence, rashness, speculative, fearless in trade and love.

When understood to represent *advantage*, the synonyms are: Gain, profit, money, success, thanks, favor, benefit, ascendancy, power, empire, authority, government, rule, glory, reputation, happy results, profitable end, victory, cure, fulfillment, termination, satisfaction.

Reversed: When this card comes up reversed it portends dire mishaps and abject despoliation with its concomitant poverty. In view of this immense difference in the value and signification of this card in both positions, too much care cannot be taken to mark the way in which it emerges.

In its modified signification of *delay*, its synonyms are: Sent back, suspension, variation, wavering, slowness, relenting, obstacle, impediment, misfortune, adversity, accidental injuries, miscarriage.

But viewed in its more bitter light as *spoliation* and *poverty*, its synonyms are: Destitution, violence, ruin, victim of robbery, a fall, ruined honor, bankruptcy, privation, violated chastity, defrauded, swindled, victimized, hopeless, sold out, separation.

EIGHT

Upright: In its natural position this card is accepted as representing either *the country* or *riches*, as its signification is relatively determined from its surroundings.

In its signification as *the country*, thereby meaning not only a rural district but the characteristics of a country existence, the interpretation of this card offers a large number of synonyms: Field labor, agriculture, cultivation, farming, garden, prairie, woods, shades, pleasure, enjoyment, diversion, pastime, amusement, rejuvenation, rural sports, rustic dances, peace, calmness, natural tranquility, rural life, forests, mountains, flocks, herds, shepherd, moral quietude.

As the synonym of *riches*, as they are signified by this card in contradistinction to others, we have: Augmentation of wealth, increase of estate, advancement, prosperity, general success, happiness, goodness, felicity, beauty, embellishment.

Reversed: In this condition the primary signification of this card is *sorrow* and *movement*. The synonyms for *sorrow* are: Sadness, affliction, grief, displeasure, desolation, mortification, bad humor, melancholy, the blues, hypochondria, vexation, trouble.

But with the word *movement*, we have more trouble in applying its actual signification, as shown in the cards, and therefore the interpreter is left in a greater degree to his or her own judgment in deciphering the connection which should bind the oracle to a specific and intelligent reading.

The most applicable synonyms would therefore be: To walk, step forward, move about, to contemplate, to make advances, to undertake, to offer proposals, to promenade, to tender offers, to inaugurate a scheme, to further any claims.

SEVEN

Upright: This is most commonly termed the *conversation* card, while it also designates the approaching receipt of some *good news*. When used as the *conversation* card, its synonyms are: Talk, words, matter, tattle, gossip, anecdote, rambling remarks, table or small talk, spicy conversation, salty language.

Secondary to this signification, and in intimate connection, it denotes *good news*, and when signifying this the synonyms are: Announcement, newspaper, intelligence, advice, warning, advertisement, teaching, history, myths and fables, admonition, remarks.

Reversed: This card, when emerging reversed, is capable of receiving several interpretations. The general one is *birth*, or the origin of things, and it has as synonyms: Creation, primitive, extraction, origin, premises for argument, cause or reason for, early, race, posterity, prime, house, family, lineage, source, commencement.

Another common designation is a *great deal* or large quantity, which qualifies those cards next to it. For example, should it come before the *ten of spades, reversed*, or the *ten of clubs*, it will mean a great deal of jealousy, or of wealth.

When coming next to cards which relate to a military man or public official, it signifies *declaration*, whose synonyms would consequently be: Orders, designation, confession, discovery, revelation, authenticity, disclosure, publication, approbation, placard.

Hearts

KING

Upright: The primary significations of this card are a *blond man* and a *man of note*. Its secondary significations are those attached to the state and *legislation*.

Representing an individual consultant, it shows a basically good man who is kind-hearted. He is amorous, rash, and a man on the move.

Coming out as a *blond man*, it has these synonyms: Honesty, virtue, integrity, fair-minded, above-board, free from fraud, upright, faithful.

Considering this card as a *man of note* or a statesman, the synonyms are: Lawyer, legislator, politician, public rights, laws, decrees, natural right, statutes, commandments, institution, code, moral law, right of nations, constitution, civil law, religious law.

Reversed: Coming out in a reversed position, this card denotes a light-complexioned man. He has dark brown hair and hazel eyes, has a quick temper, gullible, easily imposed upon, not overly passionate yet addicted to vice and incapable of moral restraints.

Its other primary significations are a *teacher*, or a *man in anger*, the opposite of the good qualities attributed to the card when upright. In this case the synonyms are: Indignation, rage, wrath, irritation, violence, atrocity, outrage, blasphemy, resentment, animosity, peril, fury, hatred, vengeance, inhumanity, agitation, frenzy, aversion, cruelty, antipathy, storm, tempest, affront, offend, mean.

The chief secondary signification of this is a *man in office*, or politician, to which these synonyms apply: Injustice, a dishonorable person, pillage, steal, exaction, dishonest man, criminal, thief, man of position or rank, burglar.

QUEEN

Upright: This card denotes a blonde who is very affectionate and faithful. She is always the closest friend or dearest relative of the person consulting the oracle. As such, the synonyms attached to this card are all good: Honesty, virtue, wisdom, beauty, true, trustworthy.

The card is also taken to be symbolic of *friendship*, the synonyms being: Affection, benevolence, intimacy, tenderness, sympathetic, cohesion, conformity, agreeable, kindly, fraternity, harmonious.

Another important secondary signification is *justice*, with these synonyms: Fairness, law, right, rectitude, fair minded, equality.

A further secondary signification is *temperance*, with the following synonyms: Moderation, patience, abstinence, sobriety, frugality, chastity, reconciliation, respect, consolation, alleviation, conciliation.

Reversed: This card designates a fair woman with brown hair and gray eyes. She is the meddlesome type who intervenes to prevent marriage. It also represents the wife of a politician or man in office, a woman of doubtful character, a prostitute, and an unfaithful wife. In this respect, its secondary signification is *dissension* and these synonyms are applicable to it: conspiracy, sedition, vanity, moral wrong, seduction, disputes, rebellion, outrage, dishonorable proposals.

JACK

Upright: As a representative card, this designates a blond bachelor, well educated, easygoing and lucky in life and love. Consequently, when the card is drawn by a young girl, and the marriage card comes near it, then she is supposed to marry such a man, and the marriage will be a long and happy experience for her.

It also denotes a soldier or a traveler, and should it come up in the oracle, in a secondary connection, it means that the person is about to take a trip. If it is surrounded by good cards, the trip will be prosperous. But should the *eight of spades* come near it, it will end with an illness. If the *ten of spades*, the trip will be accompanied by tears.

In this secondary capacity, the synonyms are: Highway, lane, pathway, airplane, car, bus, train, walk, career, a course, promenade, messenger, expedient, method, enterprise.

Reversed: Should this card come out in the oracle of

a single girl, it is a warning that her lover or intended mate is wooing her for strictly selfish rea-
sons. Although he may be handsome, intelligent,
and very accomplished, the couple will be mis-
matched.

It warns a married woman or a widow that
someone, playing the part of a friend, is thinking
of ways to hurt her. If this card falls near the
ace of spades, it signifies almost immediate desertion by a lover, husband, or supposedly close
friend.

Consequently, in a secondary capacity, it has
taken the connotation of *evil desires* or *longing*,
and has synonyms such as: Passion, flattery, adula-
tion, lechery, fall, cajolery, to fawn over, hunger
for, lust.

ACE

Upright: The principal signification of this card is
the house. As such it obtains a secondary capacity
of an extensive nature, expressed in the following
synonyms: Home, housekeeping, tavern, hotel,
motel, burial, monastery, inn, tent, palace, dwelling, lodging, shop, domicile, manor, pavilion, vase,
household, economy, saving, store, barracks, castle,
retreat, family, lineage, ancestry, asylum, grave,
posterity.

The card also designates a *feast* when, secondar-
ily, it assumes synonyms of this nature: Merrymaking, party, invitation, sports, festivity, gaiety,
guests, nutrition, hilarity, joy, fun, table.

Reversed: This card primarily signifies *forced* or *constrained fun*, but it should more often be taken to
mean *new acquaintances*. From this we derive a
secondary significance of fresh news, with these
synonyms: New instructions, index, forewarning,

prediction, prophecy, divination, novelty, enlightenment, conjecture, prognostication, presentment.

It also is indicative of a *disordered household*, and from this comes the secondary meaning of *domestic quarrels*. The following synonyms predominate: Misunderstanding, remorse, family feuds, dissension, uncertainty, marriage problems, repentance, regret, agitation, domestic strife.

At times this card even represents *family vices*, or extravagance in expenditures. It also can be used to describe crime or folly which renders the home unendurable and extremely unhappy.

TEN

Upright: This card ordinarily signifies the *city*, and its secondary capacities are expressed in some of the following synonyms: Native land, community, borough, town, metropolis, village, locality, habitation, dwelling, citizens, city government, site, residence.

It moreover is accepted as denoting *envious people*, which would be covered well by the following synonyms: Jealousy, vexation from successes of others, a grudge, suspicious, apprehensive, zealously careful, solicitous, cautious, wary.

Reversed: This card generally signifies an *inheritance*, and its synonyms are: Legacy, dowry, will, heir, to bequeath, to endow, donation, gift, patrimony, estate, heritage, revenue.

It is likewise often used to signify *relatives* when used in its secondary capacity. If extended to its widest scope it will cover such things as: family, ancestors, father, blood lines, mother, brother, sister, aunt, uncle, race, love intrigues, affinity, male or female, cousin, lineage, alliance.

Another primary signification of this card is

surprise, generally a bad one. It carries these synonyms: Misunderstanding, cheat, miracle, wonderful, strange, trickery, deceit, troubles, fright, fear, terror, astonishment, alarm, rapture, emotion, exhaustion, phenomenon, oversight, mistake, error, vexation, annoyance, consternation.

NINE

Upright: This card always foretells good fortune, wealth, happiness and success in all endeavors. Its principal signification is *victory*, and some of the synonyms are: Advantage, gain, majesty, pomp, show, riches, furniture, attire, trophies, triumph, material goods, winning.

Its next major meaning is *union* and *harmony*, with several secondary significations related such as: musical tastes, happiness, discretion, moderation, patience, calmness, frugality, chastity, continence.

It also designates *labor* and *commerce*, in which capacity its significations are expressed in these synonyms: Merchant, trader, clerk, laborer, businessman, occupation, travel, toil, reflection, studious, trade, employment, profession, meditation.

Still another signification is a *gift*; therefore we have: Present, generosity, benefit, gratification, service, helpful, thoughtful.

Reversed: This card means *ennui* or boredom, with secondary attributes expressed in these synonyms: Weariness, discontent, disgust, aversion, listless, affliction, lack of energy, lack of spirit, displeasure.

It moreover is employed to signify *curiosity*, therefore we have a secondary signification of: Inquisitiveness, busybody, intruder, meddlesome, interference, tampering, nosy.

Then again an ordinary signification is *obstacle*

or *hindrance*, with the following synonyms: Opposition, bar, contain, stop, hold back, restrain, vacillation, perplex, impediment, difficulty, inconvenience, trouble, problems, distress.

EIGHT

Upright: The primary signification of this card is, first, a young blond girl, gentle-mannered, of good disposition, lively, full of natural ability and personal beauty. The following synonyms fit her: Modesty, bashful, shy, timidity, honesty, virtuous, mildness, fear of scandal, retiring disposition, graceful, easygoing.

It also signifies *success in expectations*, that is, in everything the consultant desires. The secondary meanings are: Fortunate, victory, cure, recovery, accomplishment, termination of pain, end of torment, discontinuance, happy, winning.

Reversed: When used to represent an individual, it designates a light-complexioned single girl with chestnut-brown hair and a good disposition. She has been spoiled by feelings of superiority. From this we find that *arrogance* is a major signification, thus: Quarreling, disturbance, noise, bickering, arguments, fights, disputes, litigations.

The most general signification of this card is *great joy*, otherwise expressed in these synonyms: Contentment, happiness, rapture, enthusiasm, harmony, exhilaration, ecstasy, satisfaction, pleasure.

Other cards influence this one and change the meaning to a *means of achieving satisfaction*, such as: Dancing, gaiety, fun, poetry, family reunion, romances, parties, balls, gala events, excursions.

SEVEN

Upright: When this card emerges in its natural position, its primary signification is that of *thought*, an *arm*, or a *jewel*. Representing *thought*, it has many secondary significations: The soul, intelligence, ideas, memory, comprehension, designs, desires, resolution, meditation, premeditation, reflection, sentiment, philosophy, wisdom, intentions.

This card also signifies *solitude* and obtains secondary significations such as: Seclusion, alone, retreat from society, exile, abandonment, banishment, quietness, hermitage.

Reversed: When this card comes reversed, one primary signification is a *package*, bundle, gift, new clothing, etc., in accordance with the interpretation of the cards immediately preceding or following it.

Nevertheless, its ordinary meaning is *desire*, or a powerful longing for a person or thing. This again is qualified by those cards accompanying it. By a simple change in the position of the cards, *desire* may be changed to *aversion*, and *attraction* into *repulsion*.

When its signification is *desire*, the synonyms will be: Coveting, passion for good or bad things, inclination, jealous, hankering, want, lusting, wish, craving, appetite, hunger, fancy for.

It can be readily seen that the term *desire* is employed as being antagonistic to true love or legitimate passion in its holy and righteous plane.

Spades

KING

Upright: Used as a representative card, it denotes a very dark-complexioned man with black, piercing eyes and dark hair. He is extremely passionate, proud, ambitious, and successful in most of his goals. If this card were to come up in the reversed position, he would be totally crushed into obscurity.

Since it is upright in this case, the card is divested of this personal and destructive characteristic. It denotes a professional man of stature, a lawyer, judge, counselor, congressman, orator, statesman, diplomat, doctor, etc.

If the consultant happens to be a single girl, this card tells her that one of her admirers is a man of great integrity and honorable intentions, that is, if the *king of diamonds* also comes out upright. It indicates that a married woman's honor and property will be protected by an honest lawyer or friend, who will save her from the machinations of enemies or those who attempt to take advantage of her. It shows a widow that her next marriage will be to a man of stature who will make her extremely happy for the rest of her life.

Reversed: Signifies a widower and a man in trouble of some sort. He is a rather heavy drinker and loses his temper often and easily. Generally speaking, this card represents a *wicked* man, and through induction, *wickedness*.

In this case, the secondary significations can be gleaned from these synonyms: Perversity, cruelty, harsh, unendurable, hateful, innate wickedness, criminal, inhuman, atrocious.

It also is regarded as a card which forewarns you of impending *disaster*, brought forth by one of the following causes: Prejudice, theft, violence, corruption, reverses, slander, moral disorder, malice, exposure of secrets, debauchery, treachery, elopement, desertion.

QUEEN

Upright: Representing an individual, this card denotes a dark woman with dark hair and eyes. She has a generous way about her and is quite candid about everything. Flattery and social climbing will have an adverse effect on her personality. If she is beautiful, then her chastity will always be in danger and her virginity can only be saved through morals, self-respect, and a strong will.

The card also indicates a widow, without respect to color or social stature. It simply signifies *widowhood* and can be interpreted as: Famine, poverty, deprivation, absence, scarcity, abstinence, sterility.

It is frequently used to denote *well-founded distrust*, and secondary significations will be: Legitimate fear, merited doubts, timidity, reluctance, bashfulness, retirement, reticence, shyness.

Reversed: Representing an individual, this card denotes a widow who is looking for a new mate. It also designates a dark-complexioned, very passionate woman who will not hesitate to ignore the normal restrictions society places on her actions.

Generally, the card is assumed to signify a *crafty, evil-minded female*, and can be interpreted as: Malice, cunning, frolic, bigotry, lewdness, wantonness, shameless, pranks, wildness, hypocrisy, prostitute.

In matters pertaining to marriage, the card denotes difficulties and impediments. The marriage will be prevented either by her own loose activities or the machinations of another woman.

JACK

Upright: Representing an individual, this card designates a dark single fellow who is most obliging. He often goes out of his way to help a friend in need even if this might hurt him in the process.

The primary signification, however, is *messenger*. This term could be interpreted as: Envoy, employed in a capacity of trust, bearing intelligence information, a go-between in intrigues.

This card is often used to designate a *critic*, or a critical position, an impending danger, an awkward predicament, a delicate circumstance, an unfortunate situation, a threatened calamity.

Reversed: An evil omen to lovers, this card forewarns you of a betrayal. Behavior and plans will be exposed by a corrupt friend or a meddlesome outsider.

Its primary signification is that of a *spy*, and can be interpreted as: Overseer, investigation, inquirer, busybody, nosy, scrutiny, examination, report, watcher, observer, spectator, remarks, notations.

Another secondary implication of this card is that of *traitor*. Here we can obtain the following synonyms: Deception, disloyalty, conspiracy, breach of trust, disguise, prevarication, stratagem, imposture, falsehood, breach of confidence, liar, cheat.

This card also forewarns lovers that if they elope, they are in danger of pursuit.

ACE

Upright: This card, when intervening between those which represent male and female, relates wholly to affairs of the heart. When the *ten of spades* accompanies it, it indicates that an affair will be accompanied by great sorrow and grief, and that it will ultimately end in abandonment under disastrous circumstances.

A primary signification is *paper*, which can be interpreted as a will, a document, warrant for arrest, writs, subpoenas, or something else chiefly pertaining to legal matters.

Another designation is *ship*, or other means of

travel by water. This is particularly true when
accompanied by the *eight of clubs, reversed*, which
means that the consultant is preparing for a sea
voyage or some other journey over water.

Reversed: When this card comes up in the oracle of
a married woman, it denotes *pregnancy*. The closer
the card comes to the one representing her, the
sooner the pregnancy. Synonyms used for this are:
Childbirth, maternity, conception, accouchement,
delivery.

From the above we derive a secondary signification, and in turn employ the following synonyms:
Enlargement, fertilization, increase, production,
composition, multiplication, delivery, addition,
growth, fecundity, augmentation.

When accompanied by the *jack of clubs*, also
reversed, this card foretells death.

The general secondary signification is a *fall*, described as: Decline, decadence, ruin, fault, sorrow,
bankruptcy, ravage, error, discouragement, destruction, demolition, shame, disgrace, abyss.

TEN

Upright: The general signification of this card is
jealousy, particularly when accompanied by the
jack of clubs, which denotes that the consultant,
male or female, is jealous of his or her sweetheart
to such a degree that their friendly relations are
in dire danger. They will eventually break up
because of this extreme feeling if the *nine of spades*
should also appear.

The other primary signification is *tears*, and we
derive these secondary meanings: Agony, heart-
sick, weeping, groans, affliction, lamentations,
sighs, sadness, unhappy, grief.

Reversed: The general signification is either a moral

or physical *loss* of some kind. What exactly the loss may be is determined by the cards which accompany the ten. Thus, if the *nine of hearts* comes between the consultant card and this, it predicts the loss of his or her job. When the *ten of clubs* intervenes, it foretells the loss of money or other valuables.

If the consultant is a single female, and this card comes out near *any jack* which is also *reversed*, it indicates the loss of her reputation through false accusation and slander. But should it be accompanied by the *seven of clubs*, her reputation will be ruined through her own indiscretions.

Another primary interpretation of this card is *evening*, as a designation of points of time. This general term connoting night gives rise to the following secondary significations: Obscurely, nocturnal, occult, to conceal, on the sly, hidden meanings, hints, secrecy, veiled, masked, concealed, undiscovered, mysterious, sneaky.

NINE

Upright: This is justly regarded as the most unfortunate card in the deck. It predicts malignant diseases, maladies, family breakups, total defeat in everything attempted, constant disappointment, and even death. The primary significations are a *priest, mourning*, and *disappointment*.

The secondary significations derived from *priest* are: Pastor, church, ritual, piety, devotion, celibacy, sanctity, religious ceremonies, church services.

Those from *mourning* are: Tomb, grave, heartbreak, funeral, burial, sadness, sorrow, calamity, regret, wailing, loss of relatives, desolation.

From *disappointment*: Disadvantage, misfortunes, obstacles, hindrance, suffering, delays.

Reversed: When this card appears, its evil influence is augmented even more strongly than in the upright position. Its primary significations are expressed mildly as *failure, abandonment*, and *delay*.

The secondary significations are the most disastrous in character. The synonyms employed in this instance are: Captivity, disgrace, need, misery, famine, adversity, poverty, misfortune, correction, arrest, reverses, punishment, detainment, imprisonment, disagreements, deep afflictions, chastisement.

When this card comes before the consultant card and is accompanied by the *eight of spades*, it signifies *death*. The following synonyms are to be used: Mortality, decease, end, finish, utter ruin, destruction, annihilation, humiliation, corruption, depression, abjection, extinction, poisoning, paralysis, prostration.

With all of these sinister aspects, the influence of this horror card can be materially modified, but never completely counteracted, through the intervention of good cards.

EIGHT

Upright: This card is ordinarily one of *bad news* and *sickness*. This is strongly supported when it is accompanied by the *jack of spades*, the *jack of diamonds*, the *ace of diamonds* or the *eight of spades reversed*.

When signifying *sickness*, its synonyms are: Illness of mind or body, bad health, derangement, agony, displeasure, pain, damage, injury, accident, mishap, headache, heartache, disaster, bad business, quack, physician, remedy, charlatan.

Sometimes, however, the eight-spot is used to

denote *prudence*. From this signification we derive the following: Wisdom, circumspection, reticence, distant, reserved, prophecy, foresight, clairvoyance.

Reversed: Unlike the other cards, the reversal of this one brings a modification of its primary significations. Hence, it most generally signifies *ambition*, a passion for which we have synonyms as follows: Desire, aspiration, climb, illusion, pride, jealousy, cupidity, wish for, go after, aim higher, onward.

Another primary signification is that of a *nun* or a *pious woman*. From this we derive the following secondary interpretations: Peace, repose, tranquility, apathy, stagnation, pastime, rest from labor, inertia, inaction, nonchalance, idleness, lethargy.

SEVEN

Upright: As a general exponent of current events, this card forewarns the consultant of a valuable friend's death. This loss will cause a great deal of misery. Because of this, many interpret the card to signify a *coffin*, which may well be true when coming out with, or close to, the *ace of spades*, or *nine of spades*.

Its more readily accepted signification, however, is that of *hope*. From this we derive the secondary meanings: Confidence, expectation, whim, taste for, wish, dream, long for, fancy, humor, desire.

Reversed: This card denotes *friendship, good advice*, and *indecision*.

For *friendship*, we have the following synonyms: Affection, well wishing, harmony, relation, tenderness, benevolence, intimacy, affinity, attraction, interest, admiration, sympathy, identity, concurrence.

From *good advice* we derive, as secondary attributes: News, wise counsel, friendly warnings, announcements, advertisements, advice, admonitions, placards, instruction.

For *indecision*, the general synonyms employed are: Uncertainty, perplexity, lightness, frivolity, variation, unsteady, unreliable, whimsical, changeable, diversity, flexibility, hesitation.

Clubs

KING

Upright: Representing an individual, this card denotes a man of medium complexion with rather light brown hair, grayish eyes, easygoing, humane, honest, affectionate, business-minded, and faithful to his word. He will be personally happy with everything in life including being a good husband, a father, and a good citizen. Much of his time is devoted to making others feel good.

The primary significations are a *friend* and a *businessman*. As a *businessman*, the card carries these synonyms: Speculator, agent, banker, merchant, trader, broker, calculator, collegian, teacher, engineer, scientist, professor, mathematics, physician.

Reversed: Representing an individual, this card designates a rather dark-complexioned man with chestnut brown hair. He is not wicked in any sense of the word, but he is inclined to be vicious and somewhat morbid. Therefore he cannot be trusted for he will destroy the happiness of others and make his own family miserable.

A secondary signification is consequently a *vicious* man or *vice* itself, expressed in these synonyms: Moral blemish, weakness, irregularity, lack of manners, lewdness, licentious, speech, ugliness, corruption, deformity, stench, rotten, flightiness, imperfection.

QUEEN

Upright: Representing an individual, this card designates a brunette. She is warm, tender and sympathetic. Other attributes are wittiness, intellectual thoughts, high spirits, very passionate, socially inclined, and the ability to converse well with friends and strangers.

The most prominent primary signification is *opulence*, which is represented by these synonyms: Abundance, riches, wealth, pomp, display, luxury, security, freedom, openness, frank, candid, self-reliant, ostentation, assurance, vanity, show, sumptuousness, steadiness, confidence.

Another signification is a *parley* or *conference*, and is expressed by some of these synonyms: Conversation, talk, meeting, deliberation, discourse, dissertation, communication, discussion, speech, grammar, to confer, to tattle, dictionary, jargon, slang, exchange.

Reversed: Representing an individual, this card denotes a brunette, with dark eyes and rather dark complexion, but not dark enough to be represented by a *spade*. She is very passionate, clean and neat, a flirt and more dependent on her natural charms than education or intellectual training for conquests in her flirtations.

The general signification, however, is *ignorance* in contradistinction to the card when in its upright position. It can therefore be interpreted as follows: Impertinent, unskilled, lack of experience, unschooled, uneducated, boorish, dull, uninformed.

JACK

Upright: Representing an individual, this card signifies a man with a medium complexion, a ruddy person. He is kind, gentle, docile by nature, sedate, studious, and domestic in his habits. He is a warm friend and a faithful admirer.

Coming out in the oracle of a girl, this card is representative of her lover, without respect to color or other qualifications, for it simply denotes the type of person indicated above.

The primary signification, divested of its representative character, is a *scholar* or lover of knowledge. Its secondary attributes are expressed in the synonyms: Pupil, apprentice, disciple, student, professor, study, toil, work, occupation, labor, instruction, meditation, reflection.

Another signification, governed by this card's surroundings in the oracle, is *prodigality*, and the synonyms are: Wasteful, extravagance, luxury, bounty, magnificence, sumptuousness, profusion, liberality, benefits, generosity, benevolence, depredation, pillage, dissipation.

Reversed: As representative of an individual, this card denotes a bachelor, a shade darker than the one above, and more determined in character. It may also designate that same young man in a fit of anger or while sick or injured.

The major signification, however, is *delirium*, and the secondary attributes are: Fever, mental wandering, apathy, tremors, unseated reason, intoxication, imprudence, imbecility, fury, rage, enthusiasm.

ACE

Upright: This card is universally regarded as a most fortunate one, inasmuch as it predicts great wealth, personal prosperity, excellent health, mental stability, marital happiness, and a long fruitful life.

The principal significations are *money* and *riches*, which give these synonyms: A sum of money, a present, principal, treasure, bullion, gold and silver, rare, precious, dear, of excessive value, capital, health, wealth, prosperity, happiness, worldly goods, improvement, benefit, profit, advantage, blessing, destiny, chance, speculation, good luck, plenty, opulence.

Reversed: When this card emerges to form a part of the oracle, its popular significations are *nobility, love*, and *a present*. But in a "reading" for a young single girl, it predicts an immediate marriage to a man who is in all probability a widower and who will be considered a good catch.

For *nobility* we employ the following appropriate synonyms: a man of stature and consequence, important, great, vast, substance, renown, elevated, good quality, reputation, consideration, a nobleman.

The correct interpretation for *love* can be gleaned from these synonyms: Devotion, attachment, passion, gallantry, inclination, charm, sympathy, admiration, enticement, disposition, affection, intrigue.

TEN

Upright: When this card enters the oracle it is to notify the consultant that he or she will receive a large sum of money, through a legacy or a gift from an old friend or close relative. However, at the same time it warns that smiles and laughter will be intermingled with tears—for you will almost simultaneously learn of the death of someone whose love you have cherished.

The chief primary signification is the *future*, from which the following are derived: Posthumous, hereafter, to come, heaven, after death, ahead, dreams.

Another primary signification is *gain*, which can be interpreted as required, by any of the following synonyms: Profit, grace, favor, benefit, advantage, success, power, empire, authority, interest, official position, ascendancy, cash, finances, rise, ahead.

A more general signification is *money*, from which the following descriptions are derived: Wealth, coin, paper money, checks, drafts, banking, innocence, purity, ingenuity, twilight, moonlight, candor.

Reversed: As a general interpretation, this card designates a *lover*, male or female. Employed in such a capacity, we have for synonyms: Wife, husband, gallant, in love, married man or woman, friend, protector, to adore, harmony, suitable, decency, fitness, corresponding, cherish.

This card also often designates a *house*.

NINE

Upright: The general primary signification of this card, when employed as a measure of time, is the *present*, for which we have these synonyms: now, presently, suddenly, actually, instantly, unexpectedly, momentarily.

The second primary signification is an *effect*, and we derive the synonyms of this nature: Certainty, for sure, result, conviction, evidence, conclusion, consequence, happening, to finish, to start, household goods, furniture, personal estate, bonds, movable goods.

This card also has the primary signification of *indiscretion*, from which are derived the following secondary meanings: Rash, haste, want of fore-sight, imprudent, thoughtless, impulsive, suddenly, chaos, confusion, misconduct, disgrace, disorder, unrestrained, dissipation, moral ruination, inharmonious, headlong.

Reversed: This card usually denotes that the consultant will be receiving a gift or *present* of some kind very shortly. What this gift might be and its value can only be determined by the cards which surround this one. The card consequently must represent: Presentation, memorial, a service, offer of money, a gratification, testimonial, thanksgiving.

Another important signification of this card is *gambling*, and the following meanings are derived from it: Card playing, lottery, games of chance, circumstance, destiny, by accident, dice, money games, luck, human life, bad company.

EIGHT

Upright: Representing an individual, this card designates a brunette, single girl or woman. She is remarkably striking in appearance and is very easy-going and good-natured. Even if she is not physically beautiful, this female will win admiration from her accomplishments and demeanor, as well as for her virtue and sincerity.

As a general signification, it denotes the *art of pleasing*, or, as it is more appropriate, *a virtuous girl*, in which connection its meaning is expressed in the synonyms: Virgin, chaste, modest, virtuous, becoming, decent, decorous, suitable, civil, kind, courteous, polite, well-bred, accomplished, condescending, hospitable, meek.

Reversed: As an individual's representative, this card denotes a mildly dark-complexioned, unmarried woman with dark brown hair and nearly pitch-black eyes. She is very vain and cares little for the opinions of others so long as her own desires are suitably gratified.

The primary signification is *removal* or *departure*, and can be suitably expressed in these synonyms: Moving, relocation, change of residence, separation, dispersion, remote, distant, absence, ramble, excursion, flight, disdain, repugnance, aversion, opposition, diversion, incompatibility, rupture, antipathy, to discard, digression, trip, change of scenery, on the go, travel.

This card also has the signification of impropriety, which can be used in these different senses: Discourteous, unchaste, insincere, boorish, brazen, slovenly, wanton, ill-bred, inhospitable, a tart.

SEVEN

Upright: The major primary signification of this card is *economy*, or the art of spending as little money as possible to the best advantage. Consequently, we have these synonyms: Discretion, order, regularity, excellent management, wisdom, good behavior, wise administration of affairs, foresight, household virtues, prosperity, happiness.

This card likewise signifies *company* or *sociability*, in which connection it can be understood to mean: Pleasant relations, family party, association, friendly intercourse, domestic recreations, balls, concerts, theater, a gathering.

Still, its most important signification is a *child*. The secondary meanings are extended to designate: Infancy, frivolity, weakness, humiliation, depression, childhood, abject, minute, small, diminutive, helpless, dependency, abasement. These are the characteristics of childhood applied to later life.

Reversed: As a general rule this card signifies *embarrassment* or *impediment*, and taken in this light, its meanings will be found in these synonyms: Entanglement, clog, disorder, delay, block, at a loss, choke up, in a fix, perplexed, stifled, bustle, hurry, stop up, obstruct, puzzled, distressed, confusion, hindrance.

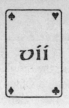

Modern Interpretations of Groups
and Combinations

Groups of Cards—
Thirty-two Card Deal

All four, any three, and any two of a kind that come out
in the deal, either upright or reversed, to the RIGHT of
the consultant—their meanings.

Four kings: Removal, or dismissal.
Four queens: Great assemblage of women.
Four jacks: An illness, general bad health.
Four aces: A great surprise, more than ever expected.
Four tens: An affair of justice, in the courts possibly.
Four nines: An agreeable surprise, but one expected.
Four eights: A reversal in finances or business mat-
    ters.
Four sevens: Intrigue, illicit love.
Three kings: Consultation on important matters.
Three queens: Female deceit.
Three jacks: A trifling dispute, readily solved.
Three aces: Paltry success, nothing big.
Three tens: Abrupt change in social position.
Three nines: Petty results, nothing of any conse-
    quence.

Three eights: Unfortunate marriage, many repercussions.

Three sevens: Pain in the limbs. General contrariness.

Two kings: Petty advice which is best to ignore.

Two queens: Friends will call or see you.

Two jacks: Restless of mind and body. Uneasy.

Two aces: Deception and deceitfulness.

Two tens: Change of a sort.

Two nines: A little money.

Two eights: A new acquaintance.

Two sevens: Trifling news.

All four, any three, and any two of a kind that come out in the deal, either upright or reversed, to the LEFT of the consultant—their meanings.

Four kings: Very quick in business matters.

Four queens: Bad company.

Four jacks: Deprived and desperately in need.

Four aces: Disagreeable surprise.

Four tens: An occurrence or event of importance.

Four nines: Another disagreeable surprise.

Four eights: A serious error.

Four sevens: An unjust man.

Three kings: Buying, selling, and trading.

Three queens: Friendly feast or dinner.

Three jacks: Idleness.

Three aces: Misconduct, dishonesty.

Three tens: Many needs of life.

Three nines: Imprudence, carelessness.

Three eights: A play or skit.

Three sevens: Great joy and fulfillment.

Two kings: Many projects.

Two queens: Occupation.

Two jacks: Company, visitors.

Two aces: Bitter enemies.
Two tens: To be in expectation.
Two nines: Profit.
Two eights: You will be crossed.
Two sevens: A new acquaintance will criticize you.

Combinations of Two Cards— Thirty-two Card Deal

Any of the following two cards that come out together in the deal, upright unless otherwise stated—first card named is the lefthand one of the two—their meanings.

Ace of hearts reversed and ten of hearts: Surprise at the house.

Ace of hearts and ace of spades reversed: Distrust.

Ace of hearts and ten of diamonds: A blow.

Ace of hearts reversed and jack of diamonds: Someone is waiting for you.

Ace of hearts and eight of hearts reversed: Money due.

Ace of hearts and jack of clubs: Flattery.

Ace of hearts and seven of diamonds reversed: Words at the house.

Ace of hearts and queen of clubs reversed: Injustice.

Ace of clubs and ace of spades, both reversed: Imprisonment.

Ace of clubs reversed and ace of diamonds: Love letter.

Ace of clubs and ten of spades, both reversed: Jealousy in love.

Ace of clubs reversed and ten of hearts: A love surprise.

Ace of clubs and seven of diamonds reversed: A great deal of money.

Ace of clubs and ten of clubs: A sum of money.

Ace of spades and seven of spades reversed: Lawsuit.

Ace of spades reversed and nine of hearts: Despair.

Ace of spades reversed and queen of clubs: Gross injustice.

Ace of spades reversed and nine of diamonds: You will experience a delay.

Ace of spades and jack of diamonds, both reversed: Someone expects you.

Ace of spades reversed and king of hearts: Hospital.

King of hearts reversed and ace of hearts: Convent.

King of hearts and ace of hearts, both reversed: Stock exchange. Gambling.

King of hearts and queen of hearts: A socially prominent married couple.

King of hearts reversed and ace of clubs: A court of justice.

King of hearts reversed and ace of spades: Campground. Government house.

King of hearts reversed and ace of diamonds: Large house, hotel.

King of diamonds reversed and ace of hearts: Ballroom fun.

King of diamonds and eight of clubs: Robber.

King of diamonds and queen of diamonds, both reversed: Country people.

King of diamonds reversed and ace of clubs: A rich farmer.

King of clubs and ace of hearts, both reversed: Loan office or bank.

King of clubs reversed and ace of hearts: Banquet hall—festivity.

King of clubs and queen of clubs: Married couple.

King of clubs and queen of clubs, both reversed: Man and mistress.

King of spades reversed and ace of hearts: Palace.

King of spades and nine of spades, both reversed: Poverty.

King of spades and nine of spades: Unjust accusation.

Queen of hearts and nine of spades, reversed: A lady in mourning.

Queen of diamonds reversed and king of diamonds: A handsome stranger.

Queen of clubs and seven of diamonds reversed: Discussion.

Queen of spades and eight of hearts: A blond widow.

Queen of spades and ace of spades, both reversed: Infidelity.

Jack of hearts and jack of spades reversed: Uneasiness about politics.

Jack of diamonds reversed and jack of spades: Strange young man.

Jack of diamonds reversed and ace of spades: You await someone.

Jack of diamonds reversed and queen of diamonds: A home-loving woman.

Jack of spades and ace of spades: Second marriage.

Ten of diamonds and ten of spades reversed: Anger.

Ten of diamonds and ace of diamonds: You will send a letter far off.

Ten of diamonds and ace of clubs reversed: Present of gold.

Ten of diamonds and eight of hearts reversed: Unexpected voyage.

Ten of spades and seven of hearts reversed: You will receive a shock.

Ten of spades and ten of clubs, both reversed: Money at night.

Ten of clubs reversed and eight of diamonds: A side trip on the way home.

Ten of clubs and ten of spades, both reversed: Loss of money.

Ten of clubs and ten of hearts: Surprise of money.

Nine of diamonds and eight of hearts: A journey.

Nine of diamonds and seven of spades reversed: Delay.

Nine of spades reversed and nine of diamonds: Great delay.

Eight of diamonds and eight of spades: A difficulty between two people.

Eight of diamonds and seven of hearts reversed: You desire to take a walk.

Eight of diamonds and eight of spades reversed: Sickness.

Eight of diamonds and eight of clubs: Moving to the country.

Eight of diamonds and seven of spades reversed: Hesitation on travel.

Eight of clubs and king of diamonds: Theft.

Eight of clubs and ace of clubs reversed: Declaration of love.

Eight of clubs reversed and ten of diamonds: A foreign trip soon.

Eight of clubs reversed and eight of hearts: Great affection.

Seven of hearts and ten of spades reversed: Loss of a small object.

Seven of hearts and ten of diamonds: You will have riches.

Seven of hearts and seven of spades reversed: Undecided about a person.

Seven of diamonds and seven of spades, both reversed: A quarrel.

Seven of diamonds and queen of diamonds, both reversed: A fight.

Seven of diamonds and seven of clubs, both reversed: Mortification.

Seven of clubs and seven of hearts: You think of silver.

Seven of spades reversed and nine of diamonds: Delay or separation.

Seven of spades reversed and seven of hearts: A good friend to one.

Seven of spades and ace of clubs, both reversed: Declaration of love.

Seven of spades and seven of hearts, both reversed: Secure, independent.

Groups of Cards—Fifty-two Card Deal

All four, any three, and any two of a kind that come out in the deal, upright unless otherwise stated—their meanings.

Four aces: Honors, dignities, rise socially—or money and friendship with the great. If all four are reversed, the contrary is true—bankruptcy, ruin, and even complete disgrace. It should be particularly noticed how these cards lie before reading them.

Four kings: Wonderful luck, unexpected advancement, and an unexpected fortune.

Four queens: Social life increased, pleasure, and amusement.

Four jacks: Thoughts of either king or queen of each suit, friendly gathering.

Four tens: Great gain, legacies, happiness.

Four nines: Unexpected and sudden news. If *two blacks* together, unpleasant news. If *two reds* together, excellent news.

Four eights: New appointments, sometimes new associations. If *two blacks* together, mourning. If *two reds* together, wedding garments.

Four sevens: Intrigues, scandal, opposition.

Four sixes: A great surprise or change. If *two blacks* together, vexations. If *two reds* together, happiness.

Four fives: A long and beneficial voyage, money, happiness, and health. If *two blacks* together, vexation first.

Four fours: A birth. If *two blacks* together, male. If *two reds* together, female.

Four threes: Period of time from six to twelve months —sometimes financial gain or money returned.

Four twos: Visitors. If *two blacks* together, disagreeable. If *two reds* together, pleasant and sometimes lovemaking.

Three aces: Great good luck.

Three kings: A new friend or acquaintance who will advance you in life.

Three queens: Quarrels, disputes, and backbiting.

Three jacks: A lawsuit or treachery.

Three tens: A rise in social life, but not necessarily a happy one.

Three nines: A sign of general good fortune unless accompanied by other bad cards.

Three eights: Love dreams, and longing for the unattainable. Wishes and desires are often postponed.

Three sevens: Losses of friendship or property. If reversed, you will never recover your goods.

Three sixes: A very large and brilliantly planned party. If *two blacks* together, disgrace and scandal.

Three fives: A delightful and happy meeting with friends you haven't seen in years.

Three fours: Strangers or visitors coming to your house from a long journey.

Three threes: Slight annoyances and vexation caused by malicious gossip.

Three twos: A good and staunch friend, but one who will sadden you with his temper tantrums.

Two black aces: Strange news by telegram or telephone, often good.

Two red aces: A pleasant invitation.

Two kings: A partnership or friendship.

Two queens: A good female friend.

Two jacks: Unpleasantness, sometimes only thoughts of people.

Two tens: Change of residence or profession.

Two black nines: An unpleasant situation.

Two red nines: A good business sign, often relating to a will.

Two black eights: An extraordinary sad occurrence.

Two red eights: An extraordinary happy occurrence.

Two black sevens: Great treachery, especially if reversed.

Two red sevens: Something sudden and unexpected.

Two black sixes: A nasty, deceitful person or a great danger, possibly an accident of some sort.

Two red sixes: A good friend.

Two black fives: Danger from falls, or possibly by water.

Two red fives: Joyful and unexpected news.

Two black fours: Separation or unfriendly meetings.

Two red fours: Good friendly meetings, good luck all around.

Two black threes: Disappointment and tears.

Two red threes: Pleasant and profitable visitors and friends.

Two black twos: A departure.

Two red twos: An arrival.

Combination of Two Cards—
Fifty-two Card Deal

Any of the following two cards that come out together
in the deal, upright unless otherwise stated—their meanings.

Ace of diamonds and ten of hearts: A marriage
engagement.

Ace of diamonds and nine of hearts: Hopes fulfilled.

Queen of spades and jack of spades: Widowhood.

Ten of hearts and four of hearts: Marriage.

Nine of hearts and nine of diamonds: A delightful
surprise about money.

Nine of hearts and nine of clubs: Something good
about a legacy.

Nine of spades and six of spades: A bitter and im-
placable enemy.

Nine of spades and ten of spades: Danger by fire.

Eight of hearts and nine of hearts: Great good luck
through love.

Eight of hearts and seven of hearts: Doubt and indecision, an offer.

Eight of spades and ten of spades: Unpleasant news
at night.

Eight of spades and five of spades: Anger caused by
jealousy.

Eight of spades and seven of clubs: Prison or con-
finement.

Seven of hearts and seven of diamonds reversed: An
expensive gift.

Seven of hearts and three of spades: A trip and a
strange adventure.

Seven of spades and nine of spades: Separation.

Seven of spades and two of spades: Treachery, scandal, and vexation.

Six of spades and seven of spades: Tears caused by gossip.

Six of spades and four of spades: Sickness and danger.

Six of spades and seven of spades reversed: A fall or injury.

Six of spades and eight of spades: Delay, postponement.

Three of diamonds and three of hearts: In nine days.

Three of spades and two of spades: Short, disagreeable trip.

Miscellaneous Combinations— Fifty-two Card Deal

Any of the following cards that come out together in the deal, upright unless otherwise stated—their meanings.

Ace of spades, nine of spades, seven of spades, and four of spades: Death and total destruction, complete disaster.

Ace of spades, ten of spades, nine of spades, and seven of spades: Divorce and many related problems.

Any three tens and five of hearts: Happy love returned.

Ten of spades, eight of spades, and five of spades: Broken engagement or unfulfilled promises.

Seven of spades, six of spades, and five of spades: Thieves or danger of a robbery.

It will be found of material assistance to the complete
to be perfect.

Modern Use of Thirty-two Cards—
Five Methods of Dealing

In all of the following methods, the thirty-two-card pack is used. This consists of the ace, king, queen, jack, ten, nine, eight, and seven of each suit, and usually the extra consultant card to represent the person consulting the cards.

When you are about to consult the oracle, the cards should be arranged in the following manner prior to shuffling:

> King of each suit
> Queen of each suit
> Jack of each suit
> Ace of each suit
> Ten of each suit
> Nine of each suit
> Eight of each suit
> Seven of each suit

This precaution should be taken for every consultation, whether for yourself or for another person. Without this arrangement, the permutation may chance not to be perfect.

It will be found of material assistance to the complete

understanding of each of the following methods of telling fortunes to have a thirty-two-card pack in your
hands as you read, and to carefully follow out the details
with the specific cards mentioned in the text. I strongly
recommend this plan to the student who desires to
become an adept in the art.

Dealing the Cards by Threes

The pack of thirty-two selected cards is taken, and a
card chosen to represent the dealer (assuming that he is
making the essay or "reading" on his own behalf). If
not, then it must represent the person for whom he is
acting. In doing this, if the consultant card is not used,
it is necessary to remember that the card selected should
be in accordance to the complexion of the chooser. The
king or *queen of diamonds* would represent a very fair
person while the *king* or *queen of hearts* would denote
one who is rather dark. The *king* or *queen of clubs* is
indicative of someone darker still and the *king* or *queen
of spades* for one very dark indeed. The card so chosen
also loses all signification, and simply becomes the representative of a dark or fair man or woman, as the case
may be.

This point having been settled, the cards are shuffled.
Then they are either cut by the dealer or for him (according to whether he is acting for himself or another
person). Use only the left hand. That done, the cards
are turned up by threes. Every time that two of the same
suit are found in these triplets (such as two hearts, two
clubs, etc.), the higher of the two is withdrawn and
placed in a semicircle, from left to right, on the table
before the dealer. The cards must all be placed in exactly the same order as they are drawn. If the triplet
happens to be all cards of the same suit, the highest card

is still to be the only one withdrawn. But should it consist of three cards of the same value (such as three
kings, etc.), then all three cards are to be appropriated
and laid in the semicircle. If after having turned up all
thirty-two of the cards by threes, and you have been able
to withdraw six, there will remain twenty-six.

These twenty-six are again shuffled and cut, and then
turned up by threes, precisely as before. This procedure
is to be continued until thirteen, fifteen, or seventeen
cards have been obtained. The number must always be
uneven, and the card representing the person consulting
must be among these. If it is not, then it must be drawn
out from the remaining cards and placed at the right end
of the semicircle.

We will assume that the person whose fortune is being
"read" is a lady, represented by the queen of hearts, and
that the following fifteen cards are obtained in the above
manner and laid out in the form of a semicircle in the
order they were drawn:

> Seven of Clubs
> Ten of diamonds
> Seven of hearts
> Jack of clubs
> King of diamonds
> Nine of diamonds
> Ten of hearts
> Queen of spades
> Eight of hearts
> Jack of diamonds
> Queen of hearts
> Nine of clubs
> Seven of spades
> Ace of clubs
> Eight of spades

Having carefully considered these cards, you find among them *two queens, two jacks, two tens, three sevens, two eights,* and *two nines.* It is therefore possible to announce: "The *two queens* are supposed to signify the reunion of friends—the *two jacks,* that there is mischief being planned between them. The *two tens,* a change, which, from one of them being between *two sevens,* will not be effected without some difficulty—the cause of which, according to these *three sevens,* will be illness. However, these *two nines* can promise some small gain—resulting, so say these *two eights,* from a love affair."

Seven cards are now counted from right to left, beginning with the *queen of hearts,* who represents the lady consulting the cards. The seventh card being the *king of diamonds,* the following may be said: "You often think of a fair-complexioned man in uniform."

The next seventh card (counting the *king of diamonds* as one) proves to be the *ace of clubs:* "You will receive some very joyful tidings from him. He intends to send you a present."

Count the *ace of clubs* as one, and proceed to the next seventh card, the *queen of spades:* "A widow is endeavoring to injure you for this very reason and (the seventh card counting the *queen* as one being the *ten of diamonds*) the trouble she causes you will oblige you either to take a trip or change your residence—but (the *ten of diamonds* being imprisoned between *two sevens*) your journey or moving will meet some obstacle."

On proceeding to count as before, calling the *ten of diamonds* one, the seventh card will be found to be the *queen of hearts* herself, the person consulting. Therefore the conclusion may be stated: "But you will overcome this problem without needing anyone's aid or assistance."

The two cards at either extremity of the half circle are now taken, which are, respectively, the *eight of spades* and the *seven of clubs*, and may be "read": "A sickness which will result in your receiving a small sum of money."

Repeat this same maneuver, which brings together the *ace of clubs* and the *ten of diamonds*: "Good news, which will make you decide on taking a journey, destined to be a very happy one, and which will bring you an opportunity to receive a sum of money."

The next cards thus united being the *seven of spades* and the *seven of hearts*, you say: "Tranquility and peace of mind, followed by slight anxiety, soon followed by love and happiness."

Then come the *nine of clubs* and the *jack of clubs*: "You will certainly receive money through the exertions of a clever, dark young man."

Following the above, the *queen of hearts* and the *king of diamonds*: "Which comes from a fair-complexioned man in uniform. This combination means great happiness is in store for you, and the complete fulfillment of your wishes."

The *jack of diamonds* and the *nine of diamonds*: "Although this happy result will be delayed for some time through a fair young man, not famed for his tact and delicacy in handling situations."

The *eight of hearts* and the *ten of hearts*: "Love, joy, and triumph."

"The *queen of spades*, who remains alone, is the widow endeavoring to injure you. She finds herself deserted by all of her friends."

The fifteen cards that have been in use are now gathered up and shuffled and cut with the left hand.

They are then made into three packs by dealing one to the left, one to the middle, and one to the right. A fourth card is laid aside (only this first time) to form a "surprise." Then proceed to deal the rest of the cards to each of the three packs in turn until their number is exhausted. Thus you will find that the left-hand and middle packs contain five cards each, while the one on the right consists of only four.

The person consulting is now asked to select one of the three packs. Suppose the middle one is chosen, and that the cards comprising it are:

> Jack of diamonds
> King of diamonds
> Seven of spades
> Queen of spades
> Seven of clubs

Recalling the previous instructions regarding the individual and the supposed relative significance of the cards, they may easily be interpreted as follows: "The *jack of diamonds*—a fair young man possessing no tact, seeks to injure—the *king of diamonds*—a fair man in uniform—*seven of spades*—and will succeed in causing him some annoyance—the *queen of spades*—at the instigation of a spiteful woman—*seven of clubs*—but by means of a small sum of money, matters will be easily settled."

The left-hand pack is taken up next, and is "for the house," the former one having been for the lady herself. Suppose it consists of the following:

> Queen of hearts
> Jack of clubs
> Eight of hearts
> Nine of diamonds
> Ace of clubs

They would be interpreted thus: "*Queen of hearts*—the lady whose fortune is being told is or soon will be in a house—*jack of clubs*—where she will meet with a dark young man, who—*eight of hearts*—will attempt to enlist her aid in forwarding his interests with a fair girl—*nine of diamonds*—he having met with delay and disappointment—*ace of clubs*—but a letter will arrive announcing the possession of money, which will remove all difficulties."

The third pack is "for those who do not expect it," and will be composed of the following four cards:

> Ten of hearts
> Nine of clubs
> Eight of spades
> Ten of diamonds

It would be explained as: "The *ten of hearts*—an unexpected piece of good fortune and great happiness—*nine of clubs*—caused by an unlooked for legacy—*eight of spades*—which joy may be followed by a short illness—*ten of diamonds*—the result of a fatiguing journey."

There now remains on the table only the card intended for the "surprise." This card, however, must still be left untouched. The other fourteen cards are gathered up, shuffled, cut, and again laid out in three packs. Do not forget to add a card to the "surprise" on the initial layout as before.

After each of the three packs have been duly examined and explained as already described, they are gathered up, shuffled, etc. The whole operation is repeated a third and final time. Only after this are the three cards forming the "surprise" to be examined. Suppose that these three cards turn out to be:

> Seven of hearts

Jack of clubs
Queen of spades

They are to be thus interpreted: *"Seven of hearts*—
pleasant thoughts and friendly intentions—*jack of clubs*
—of a dark young man—*queen of spades*—relative to
a malicious dark woman, who will cause him much
unhappiness."*

Dealing the Cards by Fives

Shuffle the thirty-two-card pack thoroughly and lay it
on the table. Cut it twice with the left hand. Place the
first cut face downward and to the right, and the second
cut face downward on the left of the pack.

Now take the top card of the middle pack off and
place it aside. Take up the three piles and repeat the
shuffling and cutting in precisely the same manner.
Again remove the top card of the middle package and
set it aside. Repeat shuffling, cutting, and discarding
cards until you have taken out and set aside a total of
five cards. When this is done, examine the five discards
to see if the consultant card is among them. If so, shuffle
the five cards well. Then proceed to deal them in a row,
turning their faces up from right to left and "read"
them in the same direction, thus:

5   4   3   2   1

If the consultant card isn't among the five cards
drawn as above, take it from the pack. Shuffle the five
cards thoroughly, deal them face down, and discard
one. Then substitute the consultant card in its place.
After placing the consultant card among the other four
cards, shuffle the five well and deal as directed. You
now have the oracle of five cards for consultation and

explanation. The consultant card will appear among these cards in its proper position.

As an example, let us say that the five cards obtained are, from left to right, as follows:

> Ten of hearts
> Ten of clubs
> Consultant
> Eight of clubs, reversed
> Ten of diamonds

The consultant has the *eight of clubs* behind him, next to the *ten of diamonds*. These two cards announce his distant residence in a foreign city. The *two tens* which are found placed to the left of him denotes that he is about to leave his house (*ten of clubs*) and the city (*ten of hearts*) where he now lives.

Dealing the Cards by Sevens

After having shuffled the pack of thirty-two selected cards, either cut them yourself or, if acting for another person, let that person cut them. Take care that this is done with the left hand. Then count seven cards, beginning with the one on the top. The first six are useless, so put them aside. Retain only the seventh, which is to be placed face up on the table before you. Repeat this count three more times, extracting one card each time you do so.

Now shuffle and cut the cards you have set to one side, together with those remaining in your hand. Count them out in sevens as before. Continue this procedure until you have thus obtained a total of twelve cards placed face up on the table. It is, however, indispensable that the consultant card or one representing the person whose fortune is being told should be among the twelve.

Therefore the whole operation must be recommenced if it has not made its appearance.

Your twelve cards are spread out before you in exactly the same order in which they have come to hand. You may begin to explain or "read" them in the manner fully described in the first section of this chapter, "DEALING THE CARDS IN THREES." Always keep in mind both their individual and relative significations.

Thus, you first count the cards by sevens. Begin with the one representing the person for whom you are acting. Go from right to left. Then take the two cards at either extremity of the line or half circle, and unite them, etc. Afterward, form the three heaps or packs and the "surprise" precisely as I have described previously. Indeed, the only difference between this and the three-card method is the manner in which the cards are obtained.

Dealing the Cards by Sixteens

After the thirty-two cards have been well shuffled and cut, they are dealt out in two packs containing sixteen cards in each. The person consulting is asked to select one of the packs. The first card of the chosen pack is laid aside to form the "surprise." The other fifteen are turned up and ranged in a half circle before the dealer. They go from left to right, being placed in the order in which they come to hand.

If the card representing the person consulting is not found among the fifteen, the cards must all be gathered up, shuffled, cut and dealt as before. This process must be repeated until the missing card makes its appearance in the pack chosen by the person it represents.

Once the proper layout of fifteen is arrived at, they are then explained, first, by interpreting the meaning of any pairs, triplets, or fours that appear among them. Then count them in sevens, going from right to left. Begin with the card representing the person consulting. Lastly, take the cards at either extremity of the line, and pair them.

When this is done, the fifteen cards are gathered up, shuffled, cut, and dealt so as to form three packs of five cards each. From each of these three packs, withdraw the topmost card. Place it on the one previously laid aside for the "surprise." Now you have four packs of four cards each.

The person consulting is requested to choose one of the four packs. This pack is then turned up, and the four cards are spread out from left to right. Then the individual and relative signification ascribed to them is duly explained. In like manner the pack on the left, which will be "for the house," is used. Then the third one, "for those who do not expect it," and lastly, the "surprise."

In order to make the meaning perfectly clear, another example is given. Suppose that the pack for the person consulting consists of:

Jack of hearts
Ace of diamonds
Queen of clubs
Eight of spades, reversed

It will be easy to interpret them as follows: "The *jack of hearts*—a gay young bachelor—the *ace of diamonds*—who has written, or who will very soon write a letter—*queen of clubs*—to a dark woman—*eight of spades, reversed*—to make proposals to her, which will not be accepted."

On looking back to the list of significations in Chapter 5, it will be readily seen that each card becomes an element, or a phrase, and only a little practice is needed to combine them into whole sentences. A further example will be given by interpreting the significations of the three other packs.

"For the house" is assumed to consist of:

> Queen of hearts
> Jack of spades, reversed
> Ace of clubs
> Nine of diamonds

These will be interpreted as: "The *queen of hearts*— a fair woman, with a mild and amiable disposition— *jack of spades, reversed*—will be deceived by a dark, ill-bred young man—the *ace of clubs*—but she will re-receive some good news, which will console her—*nine of diamonds*—although it is probable that the news will be delayed."

The pack "for those who do not expect it" consists of:

> Queen of diamonds
> King of spades
> Ace of hearts, reversed
> Seven of spades

These four cards are "read" as follows: "The *queen of diamonds*—a mischief-making woman—the *king of spades*—in league with a dishonest lawyer—*ace of hearts, reversed*—will hold a consultation—*seven of spades*—but the harm they cause will soon be repaired."

Last comes the "surprise," formed by, let us say:

> Jack of clubs
> Ten of diamonds
> Queen of spades
> Nine of spades

The interpretation would go like this: "The *jack of clubs*—a clever, enterprising young man—*ten of diamonds*—about to undertake a journey—*queen of spades*—for the purpose of visiting a widow—*nine of spades*—but one or both their lives will be endangered."

The Twenty-one Card Method

After the thirty-two cards have been shuffled and cut with the left hand, the first eleven are withdrawn from the pack and laid on one side. The remainder—twenty-one in all—are to again be shuffled and cut. That being done, the topmost card is laid to one side by itself to form the "surprise." The remaining twenty are ranged in a semicircle before the dealer in the exact order in which they came to hand. If the card representing the person consulting is not among them, one must be withdrawn from the eleven useless ones. Place this card at the right extremity of the row, where it represents the missing consultant card, no matter what it may really be.

Let us assume that the person wishing to have the "reading" is an army officer and consequently represented by the king of diamonds. The twenty cards ranged in front of you happen to be:

> Queen of diamonds
> King of clubs
> Ten of hearts
> Ace of spades
> Queen of hearts, reversed
> Seven of spades
> Jack of diamonds
> Ten of clubs
> King of spades
> Eight of diamonds

King of hearts
Nine of clubs
Jack of spades, reversed
Seven of hearts
Ten of spades
King of diamonds
Ace of diamonds
Seven of clubs
Nine of hearts
Ace of clubs

You now proceed to examine the cards as they lie. Perceiving that all the *four kings* are there, you can predict that great rewards await the person consulting you, and that he will gain great dignity and honor. The *two queens*, one of them *reversed*, announce the reunion of two sorrowful friends. The *three aces* foretell good news, the *two jacks*, one of them *reversed*, represent danger, and the *three tens*, improper conduct.

You now begin to explain the cards, commencing with the first one on the left hand: "The *queen of diamonds*—is a mischief-making, ill-bred woman—*king of clubs*—endeavoring to win the affections of a worthy and estimable man—*ten of hearts*—over whose scruples she will triumph—*ace of spades*—the affair will make some noise—*queen of hearts, reversed*—and greatly distress a charming fair woman who loves him—*seven of spades*—but her grief will not be of long duration. *Jack of diamonds*—an unfaithful servant—*ten of clubs* —will make away with a considerable sum of money— *king of spades*—and will be brought to trial—*eight of diamonds*—but saved from any punishment through a woman's plea. *King of hearts*—a fair man of liberal disposition—*nine of clubs*—will receive a large sum of money—*jack of spades, reversed*—which will expose him to the malice of a dark youth with coarse manners. *Seven of hearts*—pleasant thoughts, followed by—*ten of spades*—deep chagrin—*king of diamonds*—await a man in uniform, who is the person consulting me—*ace of diamonds*—but he will speedily receive a letter—*seven of clubs*—containing a small sum of money—*nine of hearts*—which will restore his good spirits—*ace of clubs*—which will be further augmented by some good news."

Now turn up the "surprise," which in this case is assumed to be the *ace of hearts*: "A card which is believed to predict great happiness, caused by a love letter, but which, in making up with the other *three aces*, is said to show that this sudden joy will be followed by great misfortunes."

The total twenty-one cards are now gathered up, shuffled, and cut. Then take the topmost card and lay it aside by itself to form the "surprise." The remaining twenty cards are dealt out into three packets. When this is done you will note that the first two packets are each composed of seven cards, while the third contains only six. The person consulting is requested to select one of the three packs. The one chosen is then taken up and spread out from left to right, being explained or "read" as previously described.

The cards are again gathered up, shuffled, cut, and formed into three packs. One card is of course here again first dealt to form the "surprise." Then proceed exactly as before. The whole operation is repeated one more time. The *three cards* now forming the "surprise" are then taken up and their interpretation given.

No matter how the cards are dealt—whether by threes, fives, sevens, sixteens, or twenty-one—when

those lower than the *jack* predominate it is considered
to foretell success. If *clubs* are the most numerous, they
are supposed to predict gain, considerable fortune, etc.
If *picture cards*—dignity and honor are denoted, while
hearts represent gladness, good news, etc., and *spades*,
death or sickness.

Determining a Wish—
Seven Exciting Methods

Having finished all the different methods for laying cards, let us explain the techniques for predicting whether the person consulting the cards will obtain his wish. There are several, in this order.

Wish Number One

The pack of thirty-two selected cards is first well shuffled and cut. Then proceed by turning them up in threes. If an *ace* appears among the three, those three cards must be taken out and set aside. If the *nine of hearts* and the *significator* appear, they must also be taken out along with the cards which accompany them. This operation has to be repeated three times. If in the three times the *four aces*, the *significator*, and the *nine of hearts* come out in eleven or nine cards, then the wish is said to come true. If they do not appear under twelve or fifteen, it is said that the wish will not come to pass.

To make the meaning perfectly clear, we will assume that a dark man, represented by the *king of clubs*, is making the wish. Having shuffled well and then cut the cards, they must be turned up in threes.

The first three turn out to be the *king of diamonds, ace of spades*, and *king of clubs*—the person making the wish. The next three are the *king of spades, queen of spades*, and *ten of diamonds*—these are useless. The next three are the *ten of hearts, six of diamonds*, and *king of hearts*—these are laid to one side. Then the *seven of spades, eight of spades*, and the *ace of diamonds* come up—these are withdrawn and put over the other three, with the *ace of spades* and the *significator*. The next three are *nine of diamonds, eight of clubs*, and *ace of clubs*—these come out. Likewise, the *jack of clubs, ten of spades*, and the *ace of hearts*. The two left are the *jack of spades*, and the *nine of hearts*—the other cards are useless. Fourteen cards are now left. They are shuffled and cut, and again dealt in threes.

The *ace of spades, nine of hearts*, and *king of spades* remain. The next three, *ten of spades, ace of hearts*, and *nine of diamonds* also remain. The following triplet consisting of the *king of diamonds, king of clubs*, and *jack of clubs* all come out. The *seven of spades, ace of diamonds*, and *eight of clubs* remain, as do the two last cards—the *eight of spades* and the *ace of clubs*. This makes eleven cards, so that the wish is considered to be fulfilled. But if it is tried the third time, and more cards come out, then it is supposed that it will be speedily accomplished.

Wish Number Two

Shuffle and cut the pack of thirty-two selected cards. Put them together, and turn up in threes. Supposing there should be two of one suit, and one of another— then the highest is taken out and laid on the table. Should there be three of one suit, all are to be withdrawn and also laid on the table in front of the dealer.

Form these cards in the shape of a semicircle or a horse-shoe. If three of equal value—such as three kings, or three tens, they are likewise to come out. The pack is gone through, then shuffled and cut again. When the end of the pack is arrived at, this is repeated a third time.

Now go to the cards laid out on the table and count from the significator, or if that card should not appear naturally, use the jack (which is taken to represent the thoughts of the person consulting). Seven are to be counted each way. Then the cards are paired from end to end, being "read" as arrived at. When this is completed, then gather the cards, shuffle and cut in three. Deal them out in packets of four, face down. Each packet is taken up and looked through. The cards are carefully turned up until an *ace* is found. Should there be no *ace* in the parcel, it is to be laid aside as of no importance. The cards are shuffled and cut again, and dealt out in packets of three. Then the packets are taken up and examined as before, stopping each time at the ace. The third time they are taken up and shuffled but *not* cut and dealt in packets of two, and proceeded with as before. Should the *four aces* (in the last deal) turn up without another card, the wish is supposed to be certain, and be fulfilled immediately. If the *aces* come out with *hearts* or *diamonds*, there will be some delay. But, if the *nine of spades* or *seven of spades* makes its appearance with the *aces*, then it is said to be a sign of disappointment.

Wish Number Three

The pack of thirty-two selected cards is taken, shuffled, and cut with the left hand. Thirteen cards are then dealt out. Any *aces* found in these thirteen are to be laid aside. The entire remaining pack is shuffled and cut again and thirteen dealt. The *aces* are withdrawn as before. Then the pack is shuffled, cut, and dealt a third time. If in these three deals all *four aces* make their appearance, it is supposed that the wish will be granted. If all *four aces* come out in the first deal, the answer is taken to be favorable in the highest degree. If only one or two appear in the three deals, it is considered that the wish will not be granted.

Wish Number Four

A pack of thirty-two selected cards is taken, shuffled, and then cut with the left hand. The consultant must be wishing all the time. They are laid out in two rows of four cards each, face down on the table. When the two rows are turned up, and *pairs* are found, they must be covered by cards held in the dealer's hand. Should it be possible to cover each pair—such as *two kings, two queens*, etc.—it is supposed that the wish will be granted. If the cards do not pair easily, it is said that the wish will not come to pass, or at any rate not for a long time.

Wish Number Five

A pack of thirty-two selected cards is taken, shuffled and then cut with the left hand. The consultant must be concentrating hard on his wish. The cards are to be cut only once and the card cut noted. They are then shuffled and dealt out into three parcels. Each of these parcels is examined in turn. If it is found that the card (noted in the cut) turns up next to the one representing the dealer or the person who is consulting him—the *ace of hearts* or *nine of hearts*—the wish will be granted. If it is in the same parcel with any of these cards, without actually being next to them, there is still a chance of the wish coming to pass at some future time. But if the *nine of spades* makes its appearance, it is understood that a disappointment is likely.

Wish Number Six

The pack of thirty-two selected cards is taken, shuffled and then cut with the left hand. Then the *four aces* are taken out along with the *significator* (person for whom the dealer is acting), and one card representing anything the consultant wishes to know about. If money, then the *ten of diamonds* would be selected. If about a man, *any king*. If about a woman, *any queen*. If about business, the *ten of clubs*. The *nine of spades*, which is the disappointment card, is also added to the *aces*, etc., in all seven cards. These seven are shuffled after having been withdrawn, but not cut, and laid face down on the table. Then the remaining twenty-five are taken, shuffled well, and turned up in three cards twice and one card following (seven cards in all). The entire pack is gone through in this way until the *nine of hearts* appears. When it does, then whatever number (one, two, three, four, five, six, or seven) it falls on is turned up in the seven cards on the table. If it happens to fall on number one, and that turns out to be an ace, it is a favorable sign. If it falls on an *ace*, the *wish card*, or anything except the disappointment card (*nine of spades*), the wish will be realized.

To clarify this procedure, the following explanation is given. First of all, the *four aces* are taken out. Then the *nine of spades* (disappointment card). Suppose the dealer is acting for a fair man, or a soldier, who is anxious to know whether or not he will get his wish. We will assume that he has invested a sum of money, and that he wishes to know whether it is a good investment—or that he hopes for a legacy and is anxious to know if he will get it. The *king of diamonds* (representing the fair man), and the *ten of diamonds*, the money card, should therefore be taken out. These are added to the *four aces* and the *nine of spades*. These are well shuffled, but *not* cut, and laid face down on the table as shown below.

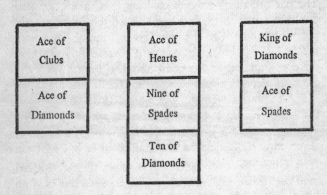

These represent the *four aces*, the disappointment card, the inquirer or consultant and his wish. The remaining twenty-five cards are now taken and turned up three at a time. We will suppose that the first three are the *nine of clubs, seven of clubs,* and *eight of clubs*. The next three are the *ten of hearts,* the *jack of hearts,* and *eight of diamonds*. The seventh card turned is the *queen of clubs*. These are all passed by.

Begin again, counting one. We will suppose that the next three are the *eight of spades,* the *seven of clubs,* and the *nine of hearts*. Three are then counted from those laid face down on the table, and that card is turned up. We will assume that it is the *king of diamonds*.

The cards turned up by threes are now gathered up, shuffled and turned up three by three by one as before. Should the *nine of hearts* fall on the fourth card the second time, that card is to be turned up on the table. We will assume it to be the *ace of diamonds*.

Proceed again as before, and this time we will imagine that the *nine of hearts* falls on the seventh, which turns out to be the *ten of diamonds*. So, in this case it can be said that the person consulting will get his wish.

But suppose the *nine of hearts* fell instead on the fifth card, and that turns out to be the *nine of spades*. That means the person consulting will be disappointed. If the *nine of hearts* happens to fall on the *nine of spades* in the *first reading*, then there is no reason to continue the three times for there is no chance at all that the wish will be realized.

Wish Number Seven

The entire pack of fifty-two cards is taken, shuffled, and cut in two packets. They are now laid out face up, in three rows of four cards each—twelve cards in all. If any *court cards* appear in the first twelve, they are to be taken out and replaced with fresh cards from the pack. Should these again be *court cards*, they are to be removed as before and the spaces filled from the deck.

Once the desired results are obtained, then start to count. Any *two* cards on the table, such as an *ace* and *ten* (ace counting one), or *two* and *nine*, must total eleven as they are counted, and then covered by the topmost card from the deck in your hand. If eleven can be made out of any two cards on the table, then it is taken to signify that the wish will be granted. If eleven cannot be made from close to the beginning, it is said that the wish will not be granted. To explain this procedure more clearly, the following diagram is given. We will assume that the initial twelve cards are as shown:

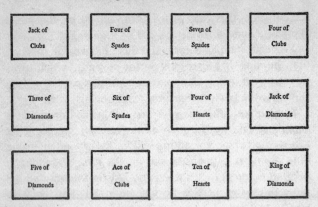

First remove the *three court cards*—the *jack of clubs* in the first row, the *jack of diamonds* in the second, and the *king of diamonds* in the third. These cards are replaced by cards from the deck in your hand, and turn out to be the *nine of clubs* in the first row, *five of spades* in the second, and *six of hearts* in the third. The cards are now ready to be counted and covered.

In the first row, the *four of spades* and *seven of spades* total eleven and are covered by the *ten of clubs* and *ten of spades*. Eleven is now made, where possible, from all three rows.

In the second row will be found the *six of spades* and the *five of spades*—these are covered by the *two of clubs* and the *one (ace) of spades*.

In the third row, *one (ace) of clubs* and *ten of hearts*, covered by *seven of diamonds* and *three of spades*. In the same row, *five of diamonds* and *six of hearts*, covered by the *two of diamonds* and *king of hearts*.

In the first and second rows, *nine of clubs* and *two of clubs*, covered by the *four of diamonds* and *eight of diamonds*.

In the second row, *three of diamonds* and *eight of diamonds*, covered by the *jack of hearts* and *queen of clubs*.

In the first and second rows, the *one (ace) of spades* and the *ten of spades*, covered by the *three of hearts* and *three of clubs*.

In the first and third rows, *four of clubs* and *seven of diamonds*, covered by the *ten of diamonds* and *nine of hearts*.

In the third row, *nine of hearts* and *two of diamonds*, covered by the *five of clubs* and *one (ace) of diamonds*.

In the first and third rows, *ten of clubs* and *one (ace) of diamonds*, covered by the *seven of hearts* and *queen of diamonds*.

In the first row, *four of diamonds* and *seven of hearts*, covered by the *eight of hearts* and *five of hearts*.

In the first and third rows, *eight of hearts* and *three of spades*, covered by the *seven of clubs* and *jack of spades*.

In the first and second rows, *seven of clubs* and *four of hearts*, covered by the *two of spades*, and *eight of spades*.

In the first and second rows, the *three of hearts* and *eight of spades*, covered by the *king of spades* and *nine of spades*.

In the first and second rows, *two of spades* and *nine of spades*, covered by the *one (ace) of hearts* and *six of diamonds*.

In the first row, again, the *one (ace) of hearts* and *ten of diamonds*, covered by the *two of hearts* and *six of clubs*.

In the first and third rows, *five of clubs* and *six of clubs*, covered by the *nine of diamonds* and *queen of hearts*.

In the first and second rows, *five of hearts* and *six of*

diamonds, covered by the *king of clubs* and *eight of clubs*. Then in the second row, the *eight of clubs* and *three of clubs*—as there is only one card remaining in the dealer's hand (the *queen of spades*), and three other cards on the table yet to be covered, those put aside at first are taken up.

The last two to be covered are the *nine of diamonds* and the *two of hearts*, covered by the *jack of diamonds* and the *jack of clubs*. In this case the wish is supposed to be realized. But in some cases it will be found that the number eleven has not been made up in two cards. Then it is taken that the wish may either be delayed or not fulfilled at all.

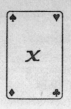

X

The Way to Tell a Fortune—
Seven Unique Methods

On the Question of Marriage

This example illustrates the twenty-one card deal and the expert fortuneteller's method of constructing a complete and connected "reading" of the same. You are advised to carefully consider this as a guide for your own use in delivering an intelligent, interesting, and coherent oracle in all cases where you are rendering an interpretation for others. A man asks the question: "Shall I marry the woman I love?"

The fortuneteller turns the cards by the twenty-one-card method described in Chapter 8, with the resultant layout assumed to be as indicated below:

> King of clubs
> Seven of spades
> Ten of spades
> Nine of diamonds
> Seven of hearts
> Ace of hearts
> Eight of diamonds
> Queen of clubs
> (Represents the woman)

Nine of hearts
Eight of clubs
Eight of hearts
Jack of clubs
   (Represents the man)
King of diamonds
Seven of diamonds
Queen of hearts
Ten of clubs
Jack of hearts
Ten of diamonds
King of hearts
Ten of hearts
Ace of diamonds
   (surprise card)

You then proceed to "read" the man's answer in the following language:

"You desire to know, sir, whether you will marry the young lady to whom you are now devoting your time? You inform me that the lady is a blonde. Still it is necessary for me to inform you that in order to be able to foresee whether or not the marriage will be accomplished according to your wishes, I am compelled to select a lady of your own complexion as a representative card of your future wife. Such a card is necessary for the oracle or otherwise our labors will go for nothing. You, sir, are a medium-dark man, and therefore would come up as a *club*. As a representative card of your beloved we will take the *queen of clubs*, as of your own complexion.

"Now, sir, having performed our deal and arranged the oracle, permit me, in the first place, to call your attention to the fact that you stand represented by the *jack of clubs,* and in the next to carefully observe your position in the oracle.

"The *eight of hearts* coming as it does in company with the *eight of clubs,* gives me satisfactory information that you entertain a most profound and honorable sentiment of affection for the lady, which it appears to me she reciprocates with no less degree of intensity. I have chosen to designate your beloved by the *queen of clubs,* and she is doubtless a person well worthy of your love, as the *eight of diamonds,* coming before her in conjunction with the *ace of hearts,* demonstrates her to be a lady of wisdom, intelligence, and prudence. Observe, moreover, that the *nine of hearts* intervenes between you both, but is placed nearest the lady. This card predicts a union, which is much desired by her, while on your part you regard your intended bride with a spirit of admiration bordering on adoration. Such a union will assuredly be followed by domestic happiness, by peace and concord in your domestic circle, and by a general reign of harmony within your household.

"I assure you, sir, that, in scrutinizing this oracle from every aspect, I fail to perceive any obstacle which can interpose to prevent your contemplated marriage. On the other hand, the prognostications are decidedly in its favor, for you will be pleased to notice that the *eight of hearts* and the *eight of clubs,* coming up side by side, and between you and your intended, predict success. Also take note, that there are *three tens* at your back, which denotes a change in your estate or an alteration in your manner of life and social position.

"The presence of the *queen of hearts* in the immediate vicinity of the *seven of diamonds* indicates not only the receipt of pleasant news from a relative able to give you assistance, but permanent prosperity should you continue to stay in her good graces. I perceive, like-wise, from the *seven of hearts*, that you are at this very moment thinking of visiting your intended father-in-law, to formally demand the hand of his daughter.

"Do not hesitate, my dear sir, to do so, for you will risk nothing by such an act of courtesy, as it will be crowned with the most happy results. There can be no doubt on that point, as the presence of the *king of hearts, queen of hearts,* and *jack of hearts*, coming al-most together, and blended with your new estate, assure you of the respect and esteem of the family. True, the young lady entertains such affection—*seven of spades*—for her parent that when she comes to be separated—*nine of diamonds*—from him upon her marriage—*king of diamonds*—the native impulse of her heart will cause her to shed many tears—*ten of spades*—at the thought —*seven of hearts*—of leaving her paternal roof—*ace of hearts.*

"And now, sir, your surprise. It is a letter—*ace of diamonds*—which, placed upon the last card to the left, which is the *king of clubs*, announces to you that you will be surprised by receiving a most gratifying com-munication from your intended father-in-law concern-ing your coming marriage."

The Matrimonial Oracle

In the case of consultation on the subject of marriage in general, the consultant card should initially be with-drawn from the pack, inasmuch as the couple should be represented by cards of the same color.

If the lady who consults the oracle upon a question of marriage is a blonde, she should take the *jack of hearts* and the *queen of hearts* from the pack and put them aside. Then let her shuffle the cards well and pick out eleven more cards. These too are set aside.

Then take up the *jack of hearts* and the *queen of hearts* and put them back among the remaining cards in the pack. Shuffle the cards well and deal them out in a line from right to left. It is necessary that a quint, or *five hearts*, appear in the layout, if the marriage is going to turn out to be an accomplished fact. If these *five hearts* are found at the end of the deal, or to your left, the marriage will be a certainty. But should the *nine of diamonds* or the *seven of spades* be placed in front, the marriage most certainly will be delayed. Should the *nine of diamonds* appear alone, the delay will not be a very serious one. But should you find the *king of spades reversed*, or *three tens* in place of the other cards, the marriage will never come off.

If the lady consulting is a brunette instead of a blonde, she will take the *jack of clubs*, and, if very dark, the *jack of spades* to represent her future husband. She will represent herself by taking a *queen* of corresponding color. She must always take care that the card ordinarily used as the consultant is retired from the pack initially.

Should a widow desire to contract a second marriage, she represents herself as the *queen of clubs* and her future husband as the *king of clubs*. These two cards should be pulled from the deck and initially placed aside.

Then the balance of the pack is shuffled well and dealt upon the table, face down, in five rows. Take these cards back up in a reversed manner, shuffle them well again, have the consulting person cut and then select eleven from the pack, which are to be put aside. Then pick up the *king of clubs* and the *queen of clubs* and place them both back in the remainder of the pack.

Shuffle well, again let the cards be cut by the consulter, and then deal. Place the first one dealt, face down, in an isolated position on the table in front of you. This is the "surprise" card. Deal the others and place each one face down in a single line below the "surprise" card on the table, ranging from right to left. Then turn over all the cards except the "surprise." This one is to be consulted only after the rest of the cards are finished. Read the meaning of each card from right to left and study their significations well.

In order for the widow's desire for a second marriage to be successful, it is necessary that the *queen of spades* and *king of the same color* come out *reversed*, and that the *jack of spades* be at the side of the *ace of spades* or the *ace of hearts*. Under this combination, her second marriage is assured.

Should the *ace of spades* emerge near the *jack of spades*, it will also be necessary that the *ace of hearts* come out to effect an alliance. But, if the consulting widow has *three tens* before her, the marriage will not occur. Should the *nine of spades* come out, it denotes absolute failure. Again, if instead of these cards, the *eight of clubs* and the *eight of hearts* appear, the marriage will be a great success. Care should be observed in noticing whether *three eights* appear behind the lady consulting (*queen of clubs*), for in that instance the marriage will not be a happy one.

The Italian Method

Take the pack of thirty-two selected cards, shuffle them well, and either cut or have them cut for you, according to whether you are acting for yourself or another person. Turn up the cards by threes, and when the triplet is composed of cards of the same suit, lay it aside. When it is composed of three different suits, pass it by without withdrawing any of the three cards. But, when it is composed of two of one suit and one of another, withdraw the higher card of the two. When you have come to the end of the pack, gather up all the cards except for those you have withdrawn. Then shuffle, cut and again turn up by threes. Repeat this operation until you have obtained fifteen cards, which are then spread out before you, left to right, in the order in which they come to hand.

Care must, however, be taken that the card representing the person wanting his fortune told is among them. If it is not, the whole operation must be done over again until the desired result is obtained. We will assume that a dark woman—represented by the *queen of clubs*—is anxious to make the attempt for herself, and that the cards are laid out in the following order, from left to right:

> Ten of diamonds
> Queen of clubs
> Eight of hearts
> Ace of diamonds
> Ten of hearts
> Seven of clubs
> King of spades
> Nine of hearts
> Jack of spades
> Ace of clubs
> Seven of spades
> Ten of spades
> Seven of diamonds
> Ace of spades
> Jack of hearts

On examining these cards, you will find that there are *three aces* among them, which announces good news—

but, as they are some distance from each other, that the tidings may take quite awhile to arrive.

The *three tens* denote that the conduct of the person consulting the cards has not always been strictly correct. The *two jacks* are enemies, and the *three sevens* predict an illness caused by them.

You now begin to count five cards, beginning with the *queen of clubs*, which represents the person consulting you. The fifth card, being the *seven of clubs*, announces that the lady will soon receive a small sum of money. The next fifth card proves to be the *ace of clubs*, and signifies that this money will be accompanied by some very joyful tidings. Next comes the *ace of spades*, promising complete success in any projects undertaken by the person consulting the cards. Then the *eight of hearts*, followed at the proper interval by the *king of spades*, shows that the good news will excite the malice of a dishonest lawyer. But the *seven of spades*, coming next, announces that the trouble he can cause will be of short duration, and that a gay, fair young man—the *jack of hearts*—will soon console her for what she has suffered. The *ace of diamonds* tells that she will soon receive a letter from this fair young man—the *nine of hearts*— announcing great success—*ten of spades*—but this will be followed by some slight chagrin—*ten of diamonds*— caused by a journey—*ten of hearts*—but it will soon pass, although—*jack of spades*—a malicious dark young man will endeavor—*seven of diamonds*—to turn her into ridicule. The *queen of clubs*, representing herself, shows that it is toward her that the dark young man's malice will be directed.

Now take the cards at either extremity of the line, and pair them together. The first two are the *jack of hearts* and the *ten of diamonds*, and you may say: "A gay young bachelor is preparing to take a journey—*ace of spades and queen of clubs*—which will bring him to the presence of the lady consulting the cards and cause her much joy. *Seven of diamonds and eight of hearts*— scandal concerning a fair young girl. *Ten of spades and ace of diamonds*—tears shed upon receipt of a letter. *Seven of spades and ten of hearts*—great joy, mingled with slight sorrow. *Seven of clubs and ace of clubs*— a letter promising money. *Jack of spades and king of spades*—the winning of a lawsuit. The *nine of hearts*, being the one card left, promises complete success in everything."

Now gather up the cards, shuffle, cut and deal them out in five packs—one for the lady herself, one for "those who do not expect it," and one for the "sur- prise." Lay one card aside for "consulation." The rest are then equally distributed among the other five packs. When you are finished, four of the packs will contain three cards, while the last will consist of only two.

We will suppose that the first packet, the one for the lady herself, is composed of the following cards:

> Ace of diamonds
> Seven of clubs
> Ten of hearts

The interpretation would run like this: "*Ace of dia- monds*—a letter will be received soon—*seven of clubs* —announcing the arrival of a small sum of money— *ten of hearts*—and containing some very joyful tidings."

The second pack, "for the house," contains:

> King of spades
> Nine of hearts
> Jack of spades

This will be interpreted as follows: "The person con- sulting the cards will receive a visit—*king of spades*—

from a lawyer—*nine of hearts*—which will greatly delight—*jack of spades*—a dark, ill-disposed young man."

The third pack, for "those who do not expect it," is composed of:

> Ace of spades
> Jack of hearts
> Ace of clubs

It would be read: "*Ace of spades*—pleasure in store for—*jack of hearts*—a gay young bachelor—*ace of clubs*—by means of money. But, as the *jack of hearts* is placed between *two aces*, it is evident that he runs a great risk of being imprisoned—and from the two cards signifying 'pleasure' and 'money,' respectively, that it will be for something in relation to being so deeply in debt."

The fourth pack for "those who do expect it," contains:

> Eight of hearts
> Queen of clubs
> Ten of diamonds

The reading would go as such: "The *eight of hearts*—the love affairs of a fair young girl will oblige—the *queen of clubs*—the person consulting the cards—*ten of diamonds*—to take a journey."

The fifth pack for the "surprise," consists of:

> Seven of spades
> Ten of spades

It is interpreted thus: "*Seven of spades*—slight trouble—*ten of spades*—caused by some person's imprisonment—*seven of diamonds* (card of consolation)—which will turn out to merely have been a rumor."

The Florentine Mode

A pack of thirty-two selected cards is taken, shuffled well, and cut in three parts. Then lay the cards out in four rows of eight cards each. The significator is made any king or queen that may be preferred. Then seven are counted from left to right, from right to left and crossways—always starting from the king or queen representing the person consulting (the significator). The thoughts, which are supposed to be indicated by the jacks, may then be counted from, or the house, or a letter—in fact, anything about which information is desired. When all the cards have been explained or "read," they are then to be paired from each extremity. Each pair is fully explained as it is arrived at until the pack is exhausted.

The cards are now gathered up, shuffled, and cut in threes. Then turn them up by threes and take out the highest of each suit. When three of equal value come together, such as three aces, three kings, etc., they must all be taken out and laid aside. The same is to be done should three of any suit come together. This process is to be repeated three times. Any cards that are remaining after the pack has been gone through, must be put to one side and not used. Seven cards are counted from the significator as before, and then paired again.

The meanings ascribed to some of the cards, somewhat different than those already given, are as follows:

Ten of clubs: A journey or a building.
Eight of clubs: Drink or vexation.
Ten of spades: At night time.
Nine of spades: Disappointment or illness.
Ten of diamonds: Money.
Seven of diamonds: Check or paper money. Sometimes jewelry articles.

Three sevens: A loss.

Four tens: A great social rise through powerful
    friends.

Two jacks: Treachery.

Ten of hearts: A party or gala event.

Seven of hearts: Delay or slight anxiety.

Seven of spades: Speedily.

Seven of diamonds and ace of spades: News in the
    newspaper.

Ace of spades and any court card: Photograph.

Two red tens with the ace of diamonds: A wedding.

Two black tens with the ace of spades: A funeral.

Eight of clubs and nine of clubs: A dinner or a supper
    party.

Seven of clubs: A present.

Three eights: Good business transactions.

Three nines: A loss in business.

Three tens: A rise, either of money or social prestige.

Past, Present, and Future

The person wishing to try their fortune in this manner
(we will suppose her to be a young, fair person, represented by the eight of hearts), must shuffle the thirty-
two cards well and then cut the deck with her left hand.
She must then lay aside the topmost and the undermost
cards, to form the "surprise." Thirty cards now remain
and must be dealt out in three parcels of ten cards each
—one to the left, one in the middle, and one to the right.

The left-hand pack represents the *past*—the middle,
the *present*—and the one on the right hand, the *future*.
She must commence with the *past*, which we will assume
contains these ten cards:

> King of clubs
> Ace of spades

Jack of diamonds
Nine of diamonds
Ace of hearts
Jack of hearts
Queen of hearts
King of spades
Jack of clubs
King of hearts

She would remark that *picture cards* predominating was a favorable sign, and that the presence of *three kings* proves that powerful persons were interesting themselves in her affairs. The *three jacks*, however, are supposed to warn her to beware of false friends. The *nine of diamonds* tells of some great trouble which will eventually be overcome by some good and amiable person, represented by the *queen of hearts*. The *two aces* foretell of a plot.

Taking the cards in the order they lay, the explanation would run like this: "The *king of clubs*—a frank, open-hearted man—*ace of spades*—fond of gaiety and pleasure, is disliked by—*jack of diamonds*—an unfaithful friend—*nine of diamonds*—who seeks to injure him. The *ace of hearts*—a love letter—*jack of hearts*—from a gay young bachelor—*queen of hearts*—to a fair amiable woman causes—*king of spades*—a lawyer to endeavor to injure the clever—*jack of clubs*—enterprising young man, who is saved from him by—*king of hearts*—a good and powerful man. Nevertheless, as the *jack of clubs* is placed between two similar cards, he has run great risk of being imprisoned through the machinations of his enemy."

The second parcel of ten cards, the *present*, contains:

Ten of diamonds
Nine of spades

> Eight of spades
> Queen of diamonds
> Queen of clubs
> Eight of hearts
> Seven of spades
> Ten of spades
> Queen of spades
> Eight of diamonds

The interpretation will go: "The *ten of diamonds*—a voyage or journey, at that moment taking place—*nine of spades*—caused by the death or dangerous illness of someone—*eight of spades*—whose state will occasion great grief—*queen of diamonds*—to a fair woman. The *queen of clubs*—an affectionate woman seeks to console—*eight of hearts*—a fair young girl, who is the person consulting the cards—*seven of spades*—who has secret griefs—*ten of spades*—causing her many tears—*queen of spades*—occasioned by the conduct of either a dark woman or a widow, who—*eight of diamonds*—is her rival."

The third packet of cards, the *future*, we will assume to contain:

> Eight of clubs
> Ten of clubs
> Seven of diamonds
> Ten of hearts
> Seven of clubs
> Nine of hearts
> Ace of diamonds
> Jack of spades
> Seven of hearts
> Nine of clubs

It will be explained as: "In the first place, the large

number of *small cards* foretells success in enterprises, although the presence of *three sevens* predicts an illness. The *eight of clubs*—a dark young girl—*ten of clubs*—is about to inherit a large fortune—*seven of diamonds*—but her satirical disposition will destroy—*ten of hearts*—all her happiness. *Seven of clubs*—a little money and—*nine of hearts*—much joy—*ace of diamonds*—will be announced to the person consulting these cards through a letter, and—*jack of spades*—a wild young man—*seven of hearts*—will be overjoyed at receiving—*nine of clubs*—some unexpected tidings."

"The cards of 'surprise'—the *king of diamonds* and *ace of clubs*—predict that a letter will be received from some military man and that it will contain money."

The Star Method

We will suppose the person wanting her fortune told is a widow, and consequently represented by the *queen of spades*. This card is, therefore, to be withdrawn from the pack and laid face up on the table.

The remaining thirty-one cards are then to be well shuffled and cut. The topmost card is then withdrawn and placed lengthwise, face up, above the *queen of spades*. The cards are to be again shuffled and cut. The topmost card is again withdrawn. This procedure is to be done a total of thirteen times. The arrangement of these thirteen withdrawn cards is as follows: The *queen of spades* in the center, the first card lengthwise above her head, the second ditto at her feet, the third on her right side, the fourth on her left, the fifth placed upright above the first, the sixth ditto below the second, the seventh at the right of the third, the eighth at the left of the fourth, the ninth, tenth, eleventh, and twelfth at

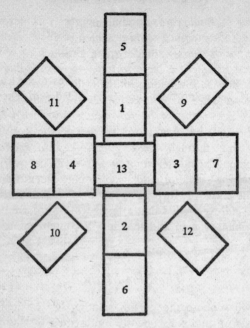

the four corners, and the thirteenth across the center
card—the *queen of spades*—thus forming a star.

We will assume the layout of the thirteen withdrawn
cards to be as follows:

1. Ace of hearts
2. King of clubs
3. Ten of clubs
4. Nine of diamonds
5. Queen of clubs
6. Eight of hearts
7. Ten of spades
8. Jack of clubs
9. Seven of clubs
10. Ten of hearts

11. Jack of diamonds
12. Eight of diamonds
13. Nine of clubs

The person consulting the cards takes them up two by two, beginning with those last laid down. The first card, (12) *eight of diamonds,* and the one in the opposite corner, (11) *jack of diamonds,* read: "Overtures will be made—*jack of diamonds*—by a fair young man—next two cards (10 and 9) *ten of hearts*—which will prove unsuccessful—*seven of clubs*—on account of something connected with money. Next two cards (8 and 7), *jack of clubs*—a clever dark young man—*ten of spades*—will be greatly grieved by—(6) *eight of hearts*—a fair girl to whom he is attached. Next two cards (5 and 4), *queen of clubs*—a dark woman—*nine of diamonds*—will be annoyed at not receiving—(3) *ten of clubs*—a sum of money—next two cards (2 and 1), *king of clubs*—which was to have been sent her by a generous dark man, who is fond of helping his friends—*ace of hearts*—it will at last arrive, accompanied by a love letter (13th card) placed across the *queen of spades, nine of clubs*—and be the cause of unexpected gain to the person consulting the cards."

Shorter Star Method

The shorter and simpler star method surrounds the card representing the person trying his or her fortune with a lesser number of cards. The cards are shuffled and cut as described previously. The topmost card is withdrawn. We will assume that the center card is the *jack of clubs,* representing a dark young man. The first topmost one proves to be the *ace of clubs* and is placed above the head of the *jack.* The second, the *eight of hearts,* is

placed at his feet. The third, the *jack of diamonds*, at
his right. The fourth, the *queen of spades*, at his left.
These cards are now "read" as: "*Ace of clubs*—you
will soon receive a letter which will give you much
pleasure—*eight of hearts*—from a fair girl—*jack of
diamonds*—and a man in uniform—*queen of spades*—
and a malicious widow will try to hurt you because of it."

Unusual Games with Cards—
Six Different Variations

Lover's Hearts

Not more than four people may play this game at the
same time, but three can play by making a dummy hand.
It is played exactly the same way in every game. The
queen, which is called Venus, is above (higher in value)
the other cards. The *ace* stands for one. *Hearts* must
be led off by the person next to the dealer. The one who
gets the most tricks this way (each making up his own—
no partnerships) is supposed to have the most lovers.
The *king of hearts* and *queen of hearts* in one hand is
said to denote matrimony soon. But woe to the unlucky
one who gets no tricks at the deal, or does not hold a
heart in her hand. To them are ascribed misfortune in
love and many years before marriage.

Lover's Lottery

Let each one present deposit any sum agreed on, or a
certain number of counters or chips, in the pool. Put
a complete pack of well shuffled cards in a bag. Let
the persons stand in a circle and hand the bag around.
Each player draws three cards.

Pairs of any kind are supposed to be omens of some good fortune about to occur to the one drawing them. He also gets back the sum deposited in the pool.

The *king of hearts* is made the god of love, and claims double from the pool. This card professes to give a faithful lover to the one who has the good fortune to draw him. If *Venus*, the *queen of hearts*, is with him, it is the conquering prize, and clears the pool. *Fives* and *nines* are interpreted as misfortunes. The player drawing *fives* or *nines* must again pay the agreed sum to the pool as a forfeit, besides the usual amount at the start of each new game. *Three nines* coming out in one draw from the bag is supposed to predict that a girl will surely be an old maid. If she draws *three fives*, it means a bad husband is in her future.

Matrimony

Let three, five, or seven women stand in a circle, and draw one card out of a bag. She who gets the *highest card* will be the first married of the group, whether or not she happens to be presently married, single, or a widow. The one who draws the *lowest card* has the longest time to wait for her wedding day. She who draws the *ace of spades* will never bear the name of wife. She who draws the *nine of hearts* will, to her sorrow, have one lover too many.

Cupid's Pastime

This game is a favorite because it always seems to amuse everyone playing it, and at the same time it is supposed that some curious particulars may be learned concerning the future fates of the consultants. Several may play this game.

Nine cards are left face down on the table so that they are not exposed to the view of the players. Each person puts a small sum in the pool—the dealer double. The *ace of diamonds* is made the principal *ace* card, and takes all other aces, the *king of diamonds* takes all other *kings*, etc. *Twos* and *threes* in a hand are said to indicate good luck. *Fours* denote a continuance in the present state. *Fives* tell of trouble. *Sixes* predict profit and *sevens*, worries. *Eights* mean disappointments while *nines* indicate surprises. *Tens* denote settlements and *jacks* are indicative of sweethearts. *Kings* and *queens* denote friends and acquaintances while the *ace of spades* tells of death. The *ace of clubs* shows a letter, and the *ace of diamonds* with a *ten of hearts* tell of marriage.

The *ace of diamonds* is played first. Should it be among the nine on the table, the dealer then calls for the *queen of hearts*. If the *queen* conquers, then the person who played her will be married that year without doubt, although it may perhaps seem unlikely at the time. But if instead the player loses her *queen*, she must wait longer for marital bliss. The *ace* and *queen* being called, the rest of the cards go in rotation. *Kings* take *queens, queens* take *jacks*, and so on. The more tricks taken, the more money the winner gets off the board or table on the division.

The one who holds the *nine of spades* pays a penny to the pool. It is said that this player will have troubles. The fortunate one who holds the *queen of hearts* and the *jack of hearts* in the same hand is to soon be married. If this player already happens to be married, then it indicates a great rise in life through the means of their partner. Those who hold the *ace of diamonds* and *queen of hearts* clear the money off the board and end the game. These two cards combined profess to foretell great prosperity for the player.

Wedding Bells

You select *four kings* from a pack, and lay them side
by side in a row on the table. The person (we will assume it to be a woman) who wishes to know her fortune
gives each of these cards (the *four kings*) the name of
some man of her acquaintance who is likely to woo her.
It is usual to pronounce these names out loud before the
rest of the players, except the name given to the *king of
hearts*. This secret the lady keeps to herself. Then add
a *queen* to these *four kings*, this *queen* to represent an
old maid.

Now take the rest of the pack, shuffle it thoroughly,
and let the person in question cut it three times. Under
each of the above-named picture cards you lay a card
from the pack in turn. As often as a *spade* is placed
under a *spade*, a *heart* under a *heart*, etc., that is, as
often as a card of the same suit is placed under one of
these picture-cards, the picture card is turned from its
position.

The first time it takes a direction from left to right,
the second time it lies upside down. The third time it
is raised again to a position from right to left, and the
fourth time (the last time) it regains its former upright
position. That *one* of the *four kings* who, after these
different changes, first resumes his upright position, is
to be the happy husband. If it should happen instead to
be the old maid, then you can imagine what is in store
for you.

Marriage Questions

After having learned who is going to be the husband
from the cards above, the questions next asked are
usually, "How much will he love his wife?" "Why did

he marry her?" "What is his profession?" These questions are to be answered in the following manner:

Gather up the cards, shuffle them thoroughly, and let the person cut them three times. Then deal them out on the table, while reciting the following:

> Heartily, painfully,
> Beyond all measure.
> By fits and starts.
> Not a bit in the world.

You repeat this until the *king of hearts* makes its appearance. If it happens that, as you lay it on the table, you say the word "heartily," he will love his future wife heartily, and so on.

Now as to why he marries her in the first place: Count off the cards on the table, while repeating the following:

> For love, for her beauty.
> For his parents' command.
> For the bright, golden dollars.
> For counsel of friends.

You discover his profession by repeating the following:

> Gentleman, alderman, clergyman, doctor.
> Merchant, broker, professor, major.
> Mechanic, lawyer, tailor, thief.
> Engineer, pilot, writer, poet.

This method of telling fortunes is very entertaining at a party, especially if you do not have this book to help you find more pertinent answers.

drawn and also fasten thereafter to join at the centre

Index

Index